LIBERATED

RELEASING THE DARK CLOUD OF SHAME

Jill E. Schultz

Printed in the United States of America
Hardcover ISBN: 978-1-960876-33-1
Paperback ISBN: 978-1-960876-34-8
Ebook ISBN: 978-1-960876-35-5
Library of Congress Control Number: 2023918223

Muse Literary
3319 N. Cicero Avenue
Chicago IL 60641-9998

The content in this book is sensitive.
If at any time you feel triggered or unsafe while reading,
please CALL 911 OR contact a professional.

TABLE OF CONTENTS

ACKNOWLEDGEMENTS

To my family who have shown their love, support and compassion even though this was hard.

To Lorna Sherland and all my HeartCore Leadership and PhD7 family. Thank you for being a stand for my healing and transformation.

To international speaker P.J., your belief and generosity helped make this book possible.

To Audrey Fierberg, thank you for being my ghostwriter, therapist, friend and sounding board.

To all my friends and support team who have shown me nothing but love, compassion and kindness as I shared my story.

To all of you who have lived in shame
and thought you were alone.

"I am baring my soul to save yours."

—*Author unknown*

INTRODUCTION

*"Holy Spirit, I ask that whatever gets revealed, whatever
we begin to remember or face is never more than we can
handle. I ask that you protect us and keep us in a place
where we can begin to heal."*

—*My prayer for you*

Dear Reader,

I spent forty-one years in shame and pain. I thought I was alone. I thought I was the only child who ever acted out because of my sexual trauma. At the age of twelve, I thought I was a monster, a predator . . . so, for forty-one years, there was this dark, oppressive, self-loathing shame cloud bearing down on me and my little self.

I was molested when I was about three or four years old. I do not remember who did it, and it doesn't really matter. What did matter was how I innocently and curiously experimented with other children because of what someone taught me to do. What did matter was the story I started to tell myself as a result of all of it. I think my self-loathing started when I was around twelve years old. It started when I got caught experimenting in the closet and was told, "Little kids who do things like that go to hell." Words like that can leave a mark, and they did! A big-ass mark that took forty-one years to heal. But I don't blame the adults for their reaction. No one was having conversations about these things forty-one years ago. There was no manual to help navigate what lay beyond those closet doors. There was no one speaking out. If there had been, my life would have been so different. I wouldn't have felt so alone. I would have known that there were others like me. I would have known that innocently and curiously experimenting with other children was WAY more common than one could imagine. I would have known that I was just repeating what someone else had taught me to do. While I understand where my actions came from, I also understand their impact and how they may have affected other children, and for that, I truly apologize from the deepest part of my soul.

As I started to share my story and as this book began to unfold, miracle after miracle happened and several beautiful and brave people came forward and said "Me too." Your story is my story; you are not alone. I was honestly in shock by the sheer number of people who were like me. All those years, thinking I was alone. The brave people who share their stories in this book have struggled because of the abuse they have endured. They have fought addiction, self-harm, disordered eating, and confusion around sex and their sexualities. They have fought for their children who have been abused. They have fought their own guilt and shame for having acted out when they were children, for having done to another child what someone had done to them.

For me, I developed an eating disorder in high school that lasted twenty-nine years. I was promiscuous in ways that didn't make me feel loved or valued; I experimented with drugs and alcohol in ways that weren't healthy. I now know that it is incredibly common for children who are molested to develop destructive behaviors. But for forty-one years, I thought I was alone.

Still, even through all that shame and pain, I prayed for my purpose. And be careful what you pray for, because never in a million years would I have chosen this purpose for myself. I would have chosen something easier, something that didn't require me to stare down my own suffering in order to help others. But here I am, doing just that because I know that now that I have come through the fire it is my calling to help others who are still in it.

Throughout my healing journey, my faith and my connection to God have been my guiding light. You'll hear from contributors throughout this book who come from a diversity of faiths and spiritual backgrounds. In Claire's chapter, she says, "healing modalities are like spokes on a wheel. Whichever spoke you pick, whatever you resonate with the most is your path, and it's going to lead you to the center. The center is you." My center is my connection to God. Whatever that connection looks like for you, whatever center is yours, whatever your faith, you are welcome here. The prayers I have offered in this book are there to share with you some of the faith that has been so essential to my healing. When you read them, I want you to know that I am with you. That you are not alone. All I want for you is healing.

I've written this book for the survivors who have so bravely shared their stories, and to empower other survivors to begin to share. To finally say it out loud. My life changed in the most beautiful and remarkable ways when I finally began to talk about what happened to me and how I struggled because of it. I spent so long under that dark, oppressive, self-loathing shame cloud. Now that I've been able to speak my truth, I look for that familiar cloud and find that it isn't there anymore. This feeling is almost indescribable—the freedom, the relief, the joy, the absolute certainty that now I get to live the life of my dreams. There have even been times when I have questioned whether it is important to tell my story or write this book at all because what happened to me has so little power over my life now that it has almost become irrelevant. What is most relevant to me is the amazing life that I am building after healing. This is what I want for you. This book was written to help you get to where I am now, hopefully, a little quicker than I got there. This is the book I wish I had read in my twenties, but regardless of where you are in life, it is never too late to release yourself from shame. It is never too late to live the life that was meant for you.

The content in this book is not for the faint of heart. It is intense. It is hard to read at times. It is raw, and real, and vulnerable, but I felt that it was important to hear these survivors tell their stories in their own words. For some of them, their interview for this book was the first time they've spoken about what happened to them, and so the emotion is still very fresh. Some of the contributors are very honest about difficult subjects, including how they acted out sexually as children with other children due to the abuse they themselves have experienced. The stories of children who acted out and the stories of those who have been able to forgive those who harmed them in no way condone abuse. But these stories are complex. It was imperative to me to include these complexities and all shades and tones of each contributor's experience. This is incredibly important, but it isn't always comfortable to read. I also want to make it very clear that if you were sexually abused, your memories, your experiences, and your journey are yours and yours alone and I would never minimize how you are dealing with it or the massive impact it has had on your life. You may not be ready to forgive. You may have very strong feelings towards that person but if it was another child, a friend, a babysitter or neighbor I want you to consider that someone probably did it to them too.

Because of this, I want you to take care of yourself while you read this book. If you have support systems in place, lean on them. If you are looking for support, I have provided a QR Code to a resource section on the next page as a jumping-off point to find the help you deserve. I don't want this book to crack you open and leave you with nowhere to put your feelings, so please, use these resources. Get help from a professional who specializes in childhood sexual abuse. Tell a loving and supportive friend what you're reading, and why. I think, though, that you'll find that these stories are not senseless. They are devastatingly beautiful. Each of the contributors has overcome so much and has still been able to find grace and strength. These stories show that this is possible for you, too. The more we tell these stories, the more we talk about them, the less power they have over our lives. The more we talk about them, the more power we have within ourselves.

Your pain is where you will be able to make the most difference. It is where you have the most opportunity to grow. You can get past it if you can look it straight in the eyes and say, "You don't own me anymore." You get to create miracles in your life and for other people. During the process of gathering the stories for this book, it became clear to me that almost every survivor's healing process has been interwoven with some sort of service, outreach, or participation in collective healing. This impulse to take what happened to them and turn it into something healing and powerful is what called each of them to participate in this book.

I hope that through these stories you are empowered to take that next step in your healing journey. The work is hard, yes, but being able to get to the other side is so beautiful. I promise you this feeling of freedom is waiting for you because it is what I am experiencing now. I have a level of peace and contentment that I could never have imagined before telling my story. I've never been more calm. I've never felt more free. So I'll say it again. You are not alone. You get to live the life you deserve, a life of abundance and of peace. All of this is waiting for you on the other side of healing. All of this is waiting if you say it out loud.

With love,

Jill

If you are in pain and in need of help, please get support. Click or scan this QR Code to access the Resource Center page at my website.

Resource Center at *www.jilleschultz.com/gethelp*

Or turn to the Resource Center on page 179 to get help.

PART 1

I ACTED OUT

"As you read these first chapters,
if you see yourself in any of these stories,

I pray that you begin to feel peace,
self-love and forgiveness and that a

tiny seed of hope starts to bloom knowing that
YOU ARE NOT ALONE."

—*My prayer for you*

CHAPTER 1

JULIA

*"I remember going underneath a slide and having him
pull down his pants and touching his penis."*

I am fifty-eight. What comes up for me instantly is shame. Even the idea of telling my story, having this book out there, starts to call up this feeling of shame. I work with a therapist, and the majority of our work has been and continues to be around the shame that I carry from the abuse that I went through. And then the shame of the cycle of what I've done to other people. I've lived with massive, debilitating shame.

My first recollection of being sexually abused by my dad was when I was four years old. Now, I'm sure it probably started before that, but the first memory I have of it happening, I was four. It continued until I was about eleven or twelve years of age, when he moved out of the state.

It wasn't until he died that I learned that it wasn't just me. He had actually abused all of the girls in our family. I have two older sisters, and he abused them as well. We're not sure to this day whether or not he abused my brother.

When the women in my family, including my mother, began to piece together that each of us had been abused, we got together and did these getaways where we would combine each of our little pieces of the story. None of us had been aware of anybody else's story, of course. During that time we also found out that my father had abused two other children in the neighborhood. He was a serial pedophile.

We suspect that he had been abused as a child and that this was a part of a cycle, as it so often is. He was certainly aware of the ways in which children are abused, and, interestingly, didn't want it to happen to me. Here is a prime example. One of the last interactions I had with him as a child before he moved away was his not letting me go over to my cousin's house. My brother was going, and I wanted to go too, but he said that he didn't want me going over there because it wouldn't be safe. He said, "I don't want you over there without me there."

The reason I think this indicates that he might have experienced childhood trauma is because I remember thinking at the time, "Well, it's not safe for me being here, either." Even though I was only twelve it was very clear to me that he was implying that I might be sexually assaulted at my cousin's house. I found this interesting because my cousins had never acted inappropriately toward me. There was something else going on that I think reminded him of his own experience. This is something I realized later. At the time, my thought was, "Oh, my gosh, what a hypocrite. You don't want me to go over there because you don't want me to get abused. But you're abusing me here." He attempted to abuse me that day, but I said no. That was the last time, as he moved shortly after.

When I initially went through therapy, I had to work through a lot of complex feelings around my trauma. There's a way in which that relationship made me feel special even though I hated what he was doing. The abuse didn't feel good, but there was this understanding that I was loved. He loved me and at the same time, I also knew it was a fucked up love. I never thought that this was a normal way that people showed their children love. I always knew there was something very wrong. But this was still a way he showed love.

Therapy helped me take these two things apart, the abuse and the love. I also had to reconcile that within my family. There was emotional neglect, certainly from my mother, but also the other adults in the family. My therapist also helped me understand that there was also child endangerment because my mom and my grandparents knew my dad was hurting kids. My eldest sister had previously run away due to the abuse, and he also was taken to court at one point for hurting other kids in the neighborhood. And yet, they still allowed me and my brother to go to my dad's house almost every weekend. They didn't know specifically that my middle sister and I were being abused, because neither of us shared this until adulthood. But they did know about his capacity for abuse.

The emotional neglect and endangerment from my mother's side of the family made processing all this even more confusing. With my mother's side, we never talked. We literally never had conversations with each other. There was no emotional attachment. With my dad, there was sexual abuse, but I knew my dad did love me. Unconditionally. The abuse was fucked up, but it doesn't take away from the fact that he did love me. It took me years to reconcile this. I know in my heart that if it had just been the abuse, without that emotional attachment and the love, I would be in a much worse place than I am now. I think that love helped me to be as healthy as I am. I still get to attribute that to my dad. Without him, my childhood would have been in this barren place. Love and abuse gets to be really complicated, especially when it's within the family. And so often it is within the family.

He was only ever sexually abusive towards me. He never hit me, or abused me emotionally outside of the sexual abuse. With my mom, it was my understanding that he was physically, emotionally and sexually abusive to her. I am pretty sure that I am a child of rape. My mom had left my dad because he hurt her. My grandparents pretty much insisted that she go back to him. Once she told me that if she'd never gone back I wouldn't have been born. I know once she went back to him he was very, very abusive. She left him again when I was around four.

My oldest sister knows more about this time than I do, because I was so young. My mother also confided more in her. In our family, it is well known and understood that my oldest sister is the favorite. Even she acknowledges that this was her placement within the family. And yet, in our most recent conversations she says that she too felt emotionally neglected by my mom.

I don't think my mother resented me because I was a child of rape. There were moments where I did feel loved by my mom. It just wasn't consistent. I don't think that it was personal to me. I think that she had walls up because of her own upbringing, and her own trauma. I do wonder if there was some jealousy directed towards me because I was her mother's, my grandmother's, favorite. She actually raised me for several years. I was always considered the spoiled one in my family, because of the treatment that I got from my grandmother. I now think that what seemed to others like special treatment from my grandmother was really just normal emotional support in a family where there wasn't much emotional support to go around.

The first memory I have of acting out sexually was while I was still living with my grandmother. I was maybe seven, eight years of age at the most. I was playing with some neighbors across the street, and one of them was a little boy. He must have been around maybe three or four years of age. I remember going underneath a slide and having him pull down his pants and touching his penis. Then, his mom or someone came out and I pulled his pants up really quick. And that was that. Then I wouldn't play with him anymore. That sense of shame came up immediately. It was more than innocent exploring, because of the age difference. I knew what I was doing was wrong, because I hid it. I purposely took him someplace where I could hide it. I knew that it was wrong when I was touching his penis. Because of this unbearable sense of shame, I never wanted to play with him again. I was worried he was going to say something. I don't know if he ever did or not. I don't think he ever did. He may very well have not even really remembered that it had happened, or not interpreted it as harmful at the time, because I remember that afterwards he kept coming by my grandmother's house to play with me. I remember me saying no, and going to get my grandmother. It's actually really cute, he was very sweet and my grandmother lovingly explained to him that sometimes people simply don't want to play with you. I think she thought I didn't want to play with him because of the age difference. She had no idea that it was because of all of my shame. I didn't want to think of myself as bad, and this shame came up every time I would see him. Shortly after that, he moved away, I didn't have to bump up against that part of myself on a regular basis.

The other ways I acted out were more consensual, more explorational. I had a cousin who was about my age and we engaged in sexual play. I was the one that initiated. One of my most shameful moments was initiating sex play with that same cousin in front of friends. We had this little pop-up tent and we were playing in there and doing it in front of friends. So now there's an element of exhibitionism. There were two, maybe three other neighborhood kids watching. My grandmother came out and found us and told us to come out, and nothing was ever said about it ever again.

I also explored with one of my best friends at the time. She and I were friends for a couple of years, and it happened around three or four times. She had been sexually abused by her brother, so I think both of us ended up exploring together due to the fact that we'd both been sexually abused.

I do have one uncomfortable memory of initiating exploration with my middle sister. I asked her once if she remembered this, but she didn't. Again, it was fondling and I was initiating. We shared a bed for the longest time, and I don't remember the exact circumstance, but I remember fondling her. Then eventually, I stopped. It was just that one time, but what stands out to me is that I was the one that initiated it even though I am five years younger than her. I still struggle with so much shame around that.

When I compare myself to others who have been abused or sexually abused, I think I came out fairly healthy. Again, I attribute that to my dad and in some ways to my grandmother. I was also lucky enough to be parented by other people. All my friends' parents parented me. I had a lot of other healthy adults in my life to offset the impact of the abuse I experienced. I do consider myself very, very blessed. I didn't end up doing anything destructive to myself, like developing self-harming impulses or an eating disorder. I partied a lot, but didn't ever end up dependent on alcohol. I did some drugs, but nothing major. I experimented, but I didn't go off the rails.

It wasn't until the night before my wedding that my family really had to contend with all of this abuse coming to light. My soon to be husband and I had a huge blowout fight. It was bad enough that he stormed out and left. My mother came in to try to cool the tension down. Before he stormed out, he disclosed to her that I had been abused by my dad. I don't remember exactly how it came up but he was so mad that he lashed out at my mother. He basically said to her that it was her fault that I was fucked up, because she let me be abused. And then he stormed out. I was shocked that he'd said that, that he'd been so vindictive. He and I have had a lot of therapy since then and processed all of this, but that was how my mother found out. So that night, I had to share with her that I had been abused by my dad. This was also the first time that she shared with me that my oldest sister had also been abused. She said, "I'm so sorry. I never knew about you."

That time was such a whirlwind. We went through with our marriage. It wasn't until some time later that I talked to my oldest sister about it. I wondered if my middle sister was abused, too, so I shared what happened to me with her, and my middle sister said, "Oh my gosh, I was abused, too." I shared with her that our eldest sister was also abused. We realized that none of us knew about anybody else. I then went back and said something to my mom about us all being abused. She was confused. She didn't understand how I knew about my older sister, and I was like, "Mom, I know because you told me the night before my wedding." She realized that she had completely blocked it out.

After that, she went to her pastor and worked through some of this with him. She eventually asked if we would all be willing to come together to talk about it. She made the arrangements and paid for everything. The weird thing is, we ended up having to postpone our trip by a week, because just before we were about to meet up in Chicago we found out my dad had died. He'd had a heart attack, and was dropped off at the hospital by a friend. He had moved to Los Angeles some time before. It was 1992, and he died during the LA Riots. Because everything in the hospital system was complicated by the riots, he was a John Doe for about two and a half weeks after he died. It took them that long to figure out who he was and track us down. My oldest sister lived in California and was the one to identify his body.

This is how my middle sister and I ended up flying straight from my dad's funeral to a family gathering to talk about how he'd hurt us. I mean, you can't make this shit up. My mother and oldest sister had chosen not to go to the funeral, so they met us in Chicago. However difficult my relationship with my mom has been, I give her a lot of credit for getting us to come together so we could each tell our story.

Other than this reconciliation with my family, another huge part of my healing has been therapy. I've done lots of individual therapy and art therapy. I also did group therapy for years, and that ended up being a really special experience. There's so much to be said for community. I finally had this sense that I wasn't alone. Sometimes I feel terrible, and that feeling like I'm not alone in my experience has helped me so much, because I would never wish something like this to happen to anyone else. But it does happen, and talking to people who understand to a certain degree has really helped me process shame, embarrassment, and humiliation. Having the support of a group was huge.

I found this group through a workbook on sexual abuse. This was long before Google or anything like that. This book was so impactful, it gave ideas for activities, and prompt questions, to not only help survivors to start thinking about their experience, but also to give them strategies for coping and managing while they're healing. I think there were some resources in the back of the book, and that's how I found a survivor's group operating out of someplace that was fairly close to where I lived.

I'm not sure I would have been brave enough to reach out to this group if not for my son.

When he was around three, lots of memories around my sexual abuse began to come up. I think this is because my first memories of abuse begin around that age. It was horrible. I was having body memories. I kept experiencing gagging, and other terrible physical sensations. This is what really made me focus on my healing.

Throughout my journey, I've continued to seek healing, safe communities. This is one of the reasons I've chosen to contribute my story to this book. Jill and I have both gone through training with Heartcore Business, and again I found a community where I felt safe to share my full story. I got to shift into being empowered and feeling valuable. I want those who read my story to know they aren't alone. I encourage anyone who has survived something like this to find a community where you're able to share. But even reading this book is brave. Hearing the stories of others is already a release. Sometimes just knowing you're not alone is enough.

If you are looking for a community to help you heal, please join my private Facebook group, Living UN-SHAMED. This is a safe place where you can get information about joining a support group as well as connecting with others with similar stories. You can find the group by clicking or scanning this QR Code.

—Jill E. Schultz

Living UN-SHAMED Facebook Group
Or copy and paste this link to access the Facebook Group
https://www.facebook.com/groups/223574946905843

CHAPTER 2

JAKE

*"I remember we were playing hide and seek, and
I put my hand down his shorts. There was an almost
immediate shame.*

*I've decided to tell my story because more men need to talk
about it. More men need to talk about having
been abused."*

I'm forty-two. The abuse started when I was seven or eight. It started because my family was best friends with his family. I have three sisters and I'm the only boy. They had three boys and they lived on a farm outside of town. We lived in town, so I would spend weekends out on the farm with the guys. Our families did all kinds of stuff together, we went on vacations; we were just inseparable. One of the boys, Drew, was only slightly older than me and would have been around eight at the time. Will was four years older than me, so he must have been around eleven and then there was Devin, the oldest. I don't remember his age.

The boys used to do this thing where they would lie across their mom's lap with their shirt off, and she would tickle their back. It was sweet, just a motherly thing. One time when I was downstairs with Will, and we were in his room, he suggested I do that to him. He would lay down on the bed, and I would sit on top of his butt and run my hands over his back. That's as far as it would go for a while.

The day things turned sexual, I was playing with Drew. We decided to go into this closet. He told me we were going to hide there, and then pointed out where he thought I should hide. He kept saying, "You're gonna go over here, Jake, you're gonna go over here." And then when Will came into the closet, it was dark and quiet. He came towards where I was hiding, to my side of the closet. He took his pants down and said "Suck on this, it's like a soother."

I was like, "What," and he said, "It's like a soother." That's what we would call a kid's pacifier where I'm from. So that's what I did. It's amazing how even then, I knew it was bad. Nobody has to tell you. You just know. I knew we weren't supposed to be doing this. We were whispering, but his brother could hear us. I was kind of sucking but it wasn't at all what he imagined. He was like, "Okay, this isn't really working," which makes me laugh a little now even though it's fucked up. Then it became this sort of secret between Will and I, but Drew knew something had happened even though he didn't know what. Looking back, it felt like Will was an older guy that I really looked up to. As we grew up, he became the town jock and he was super popular, so he had that energy about him so, of course I wanted to be around him. He felt so old and mature and he wanted to do all these different things with me. I was just mesmerized by him. Part of me felt like, "Yeah, sure! Let's do these special secret things that only you and I do together." I see it differently now, of course. And now, looking back, I realize that he was also a child. It continued from there. We were always down in the basement in Will's bedroom. And our parents were always upstairs, hanging out having fun. Our parents were almost always around. He would say, "Tickle my back," and then it was pants down. It became our code word for it. It became common, and progressed from there into a regular thing. Eventually things started happening between me and Drew. He and I would get on the quad on the farm and go out into the bush and mess around. This was more reciprocal than with his older brother. We were both kids, both of us were happy, nobody was hurting the other person. We would take baths together all the time—our mothers would send us in together to take a bath. They had no idea. The abuse went on until he was about sixteen or so. And then, actually, he died.

Outside of Drew and Will, the only other time I really acted out sexually due to having experienced this abuse was with another boy. I remember we were playing hide and seek. And I put my hand down his shorts. There was an almost immediate shame.

I instantly felt shame and had this overwhelming feeling of, "Oh, my gosh, I can't believe I just did that." It's one thing when something happens to me, but now I'm the one that did it. I knew nobody could ever find out. That this could never be shared. I'd be in so much trouble if my mom or anyone else ever found out.

Even now this feels hard to say. We don't want to talk about these sorts of things out of fear, like people would think I am gross and weird and disgusting. But now when I think about it, I was doing this to this other boy to process the things that were being done to me. I was repeating learned behavior. It doesn't make it right, but I understand how this happens. Perhaps the same thing happened to Will, too, and that's why he did it to me. I was still so young at the time, I think around ten. Still, the only person I've ever shared this with is a therapist.

This is the only time I remember acting out sexually to another child where I instigated and it wasn't mutual. I've found, though, that once I started talking about these things, more detailed memories around my own abuse started to come back. It's amazing how we can hide memories from ourselves, especially of things we'd rather not think about. I've never really opened up about this experience with the other boy before, and now that I've opened this up, maybe something else will come up.

I was twenty-one when I first told my family. I was struggling with depression and suicidal thoughts, though I never had an attempt. I did two years of university and was failing my classes. I was drinking and I discovered porn. Eventually I dropped out. I was so lost, just in this constant state of who am I? What am I doing?

After dropping out of University, I ended up going to a Christian discipleship training school for a semester. Once I got out there I prayed and I said, "God, You've got to send me someone that I can talk to about all of this stuff." And within a week, I talked with someone about the abuse I experienced for the first time, and that I wasn't sure if I was gay or straight. All this garbage was finally allowed to come out. When I came home that summer, I told my family.

I feel so bad for my poor mother. Once I finally told her about it she had so much anxiety and guilt. She was so shocked. She was like, "How did I miss that?" She and I talked, we had open communication. It was hard because we loved that family. We did everything with that family. They were the last people that she would have thought were harming me. I think it wasn't obvious because I loved going over there. It was fun. Will was like that, just so fun. He was besties with my older sister. We lived in a town of six hundred people, so everyone knew everyone. And he was just this great guy. He was the president of the 4-H Club. He was so charismatic, so well loved. And then he died in a car accident when he was sixteen and was killed instantly. It turned him into something of a tragic small town hero. It rocked the whole community. Our family was the number one support for his family at the time. His death really sealed for me that I would never, ever talk about this. I would never share what he had done. Because if I told anyone, I'd be seen as ruining his reputation and the story his parents and the whole community had built up around him. I figured no one would believe me, anyway. Will was a rock star and I was some little kid.

Thinking back, there were a few signs that something was wrong, but they were subtle. I was obsessed with my schoolwork. I was a perfectionist. I was creating a front. I was putting up a wall like, "I'm perfect. There's nothing to see here. There's nothing to look at here." I was the easiest kid to look after. Anything anyone wanted me to do, I'd do it.

I also had chronic stomach pain. All through high school I had sharp, debilitating pain, diarrhea, almost daily. I was tested for Crohn's disease and colitis, I was tested and tested and then eventually they simply couldn't figure out what was wrong with me. Looking back, it was a sure sign of the stress and anxiety I was experiencing. No one thought to ask about the emotional stuff I was experiencing that might have resulted in that much physical pain. I used to buy my pants three sizes too big because everything hurt. Looking back, that was a red flag.

Over the years, I've found myself questioning my experience. Was it really abuse? He was just a kid too. As I mentioned earlier, part of me thinks he must have been abused by someone else. How did he know what to do to me? Where did he learn it? He was eleven years old when it started. Perhaps someone hurt him, and he was just repeating what he was taught. I'll never know for sure.

At this point, I don't really feel anything when I think about him. There's no emotional charge. He's dead. I finally feel nothing towards his parents, but it's taken me a lot longer to come to that point. This happened in their house under their roof. I do hold them somewhat responsible for what happened. I still think adults are responsible to know what's happening with kids. My parents are still in touch with his parents, but there's distance there now because I was honest about the abuse. It's become quite awkward. They still initiate contact with my parents, but it puts them in a really weird position.

I remember one Christmas they showed up at my parents' house for a visit. They let them in and were their usual loving and accepting selves. I think I said hi, but then I disappeared, I don't know where to but I went and hid somewhere else. These sorts of things have happened a couple of times, which is uncomfortable. When his mom sees me she'll come up to hug me, and my body has this incredible response. I'm just repulsed. In the beginning I did let her hug me but now I'm quick to put out my hand for a handshake to create some physical distance. I'm okay with my parents' journey around this. It's okay with me that they don't want to confront his parents, and are still kind towards them. But they certainly aren't as close as they used to be.

I have considered confronting them myself, but when I think this way it's usually coming from a place of anger and vengefulness: *I am hurt and I want you to hurt too.* I've never done it because I've never been able to see how this would actually be healing for any of us. Especially because Will is gone. And I can't prove it, but I do think he was abused as well. This breaks my heart. It's given me so much compassion for him. When I look at his life, he was this driven achiever. I feel like he was just masking so many things, just like me. He had so many hurts that clearly nobody knew about, just like me. I hold so much grace for him. I've held so much more anger towards his parents, because they were the adults. This was happening in their house. How were they so disconnected that they had no idea? How did they create that environment in their home?

I think adults do have responsibility when things like this happen. Bad things will still happen, and they can't be everywhere at all times. I don't expect perfection from them. But they do still have some responsibility.

This discussion about responsibility is different from blame. To me, everyone's responsible. Everyone gets to look at it. Me, my parents, Will, Drew, their parents. I'm not blaming. I'm not holding unforgiveness toward anyone. It devastated my parents. It's still so hard for them to talk about. I think I sometimes still feel an emotional charge towards Will's parents because he isn't here for me to blame. He died. So the piece I still carry has transferred onto them. I think if he hadn't died I would feel differently. But still, responsibility is different than blame, and I have been able to find some grace around my feelings towards his parents.

I look at them now, and they are aging. I just see them as people wanting to be loved and accepted. Just like me, just like all of us. I'm also consciously seeking God on this and saying, "I don't want to have hatred towards them. God, show me what's good about them. Tell me what's good about them, because I get to love them because you think they're amazing. You created them in your image just like me. They're no better or worse than me. You love them as much as me. So show me what you love about them." The more that I do that, the more I've been able to access grace. I've realized that I'm not actually angry at them. I'm just angry. And this isn't a daily thing. It's just moments when the invitation to be angry comes up. I'm actually just angry at the situation.

I've decided to tell my story because more men need to talk about it. More men need to talk about having been abused. To me, it's story, story, story. Telling these stories, looking at the stories of others, we can start to learn. There starts to be some lessons. I think mine was "Who am I?" I went on such a journey with my sexuality. I now identify as straight. My wife knows about these things, about this journey.

I was having sexual encounters with guys from around seven or eight years old, and this really messed me up. I shouldn't even have been thinking about these things at that age. It taught me to live a double life. No one could know what was happening. As a child, I was engaging in sexual activity with guys for years. My dad was Mr. Sports, and wanted me to be a sports guy so badly. I wanted to play hockey, but I just got shoved around. I didn't fit in. Sex became my way to get acceptance from men. Will was this beautiful guy, the epitome of who I wanted to be, just this super popular stud. Good looking, fun and happy. And everyone loved him. I could be around him, spend time with him, and the price was sex. So it messed me up for years. After he died, I was crazy for porn and masturbation, but didn't have sex again until I was around twenty-five. I was trying to be a good Christian boy and not be sexual and do anything. And then I thought, well, I don't know what I am or who I am or if I'm ever gonna get married. So I'm not dying a virgin. I'm actually going to have real sex. I mostly had a string of one night stands with men, though I was dating a lot of girls. I truly became a sex addict, though the first time I actually had intercourse with a woman was when I was thirty-six. In a way, I was saving myself for a relationship, which is funny because I was doing everything else. But the first time I really had sex with a woman was with my wife.

I met my wife, Laura, back when I was twenty-one. We hit it off right away and were good friends and I shared about my sexual struggles with her right from the start. We actually ended up losing touch for a while, and reconnected again when I was thirty-three. We started dating, then broke up, and got back together when I was thirty-six and we were married the same year. So she knew all of the things I was struggling with, even before we got engaged. Of course, some of this was really difficult for her. But the beautiful part of it was that she knew me. All of me. And she loved me. She could see through all of the behaviors I'd developed in order to cope with the abuse I'd experienced, and she chose me.

My biggest fear was that someone was going to know my past, know all my garbage and think, "You're disgusting, you're not worth it." And here she was, knowing everything that had happened and everything I'd done, and believing that I was an amazing man, and fully respecting me, and even wanting to be my wife. It's sad, but at first I actually saw this as a weakness in her. I was actually repelled by it. I had so little value in myself that I thought if she could love a person like me she obviously didn't really know what she was getting into, and maybe she was being dumb, or naive, or using spirituality or romanticism to lie to herself about who I really was.

After we reconnected, it took about six months of dating for me to understand that she honestly believed in my value. I had to shift from "If she likes me, she's foolish," to "If this amazing woman sees something in me, maybe I do have value." But then she had some work to do on herself, and so did I, and we ended up breaking it off. When we reconnected again she was so sure of herself, and so sure of her relationship with God and fully knew who she was. And so when she came back and chose me, I saw such strength and stability in her. I had this lightbulb moment. I needed her in my life. I wanted to do life with her. She is such a powerful woman. I'd be an idiot to mess this up.

I am still attracted to men, but I am faithful to my wife. I've spent years wondering, "Who am I? What is my identity? I've searched so hard for an answer to that question. I prayed and prayed for those feelings of attraction to go away, and it didn't happen. I came to understand that this isn't something you pray away, and it isn't leaving. I get to accept this part of me. I'm attracted to men, and I'm attracted to women, but what I get to really reconcile with are my choices. And I've decided to choose Laura. Again, there are no secrets between us. There's no pretending or hiding. We discuss it, and have even discussed me talking about it publicly. When I've wanted to speak about it, I've asked her, "How does this make you feel? Are you okay with publicly being the wife of a man who feels these things, who has done these things?" She told me that she's fine with it. She said, "My identity isn't based on what people think of me, or my marriage, or my husband. I know you. I love you." She's an incredible woman and I am so grateful God gave me her to love.

I think my journey with my sexuality has only deepened my faith and my connection with God. I spent a long time wrestling with my faith and with the Bible. There are passages that don't condone same sex relationships. That's just true. And I spent a long time trying to prove otherwise, like, maybe it meant something different. I fought it and fought it, and then would swing back to trying to prove that I was straight, and that I aligned completely with what I was reading. I just couldn't reconcile what I was reading with how I felt about myself and how I felt about my faith, and it was exhausting. Finally, I got to this level of desperation where I let go and said to God, "I don't know what or who I am supposed to be, and I don't know what you want." It was a beautiful and awful place to be. I felt like the pieces of me that were fighting, that were performing, melted away and I was able to come to God and ask "Which version of me will you love? What do I have to do? What do I have to say?" And in this moment it became clear that there wasn't a more lovable version of me. God created me as I am. I could stop fighting, performing, pretending. All I had to do was to be myself.

What's helped me heal is vulnerability, openness, and stepping into desperation. I love desperation. To me, it's this moment of honesty where you admit you don't know. You don't have it all together. You get to fall apart, and lean on trusted people. Opening up to people is difficult and messy. One of the most healing things I've done was opening up to my male friends. I've got a really tight friendship with a group of eight other guys and I've been super vulnerable with them and have shared my experiences with them. What's amazing is that they've shared openly about their personal struggles and experiences with me, too. It's not just all about me. This sort of vulnerability makes for friendships that are strong and healing for everybody. This openness isn't a one time thing. We are friends who chose each other, and we share continually. I've benefited from therapy a lot as well. I think I learned to be able to be open like this in therapy.

Getting to the place I am now has been truly hard. There were moments that I couldn't see my way out. That I didn't want to be alive. I was so scared I would never be married, never have a family, and I've wanted to be a father and a husband from a very young age. Feeling like that wasn't a possibility for me was heartbreaking. Terrifying. I had such a low image of myself that I didn't understand how anyone could ever trust me. How I could ever have deep friendships. I thought that as soon as someone really started to know me, they would run.

This desperation finally made me turn and look to God and allow him to step in. He stepped in and I got to surrender. Desperation has always led me to Him, and when I look at Him, my problems are suddenly really small. I can feel him saying, "I got you. You're good. You're amazing. My love towards you has never changed. My thoughts towards you have never changed. You are my beloved son, and my opinion of you has not changed one bit. Come on back."

This is what I want people that have gone through something similar to know. You get to stop fighting. You get to just be yourself. You are not the things that happened to you. You were created in God's image and are therefore irrevocably enough. There's nothing that anyone has done to you or could do to you that can change that, diminish it or damage it, or take it away. My experiences, while they were difficult and painful and confusing, resulted in me doing so much important work. I've built a relationship that feels strong and healthy with a woman who sees me as valuable and loveable and worthy. I've built a relationship with myself where I get to see myself as valuable, and lovable, and worthy. And I know God has seen me that way all along.

CHAPTER 3

LILY

"I was caught in a closet with my two boy cousins. Again,
I was the instigator of the sexual contact.
I was teaching them."

I'm fifty-three years old. The first sexual encounter that I
remember having was when I was five years old. I was teaching
a four-year-old boy how to have sex with me. I was walking him
through it as if I were a teacher. I explained how his private parts
worked and how my private parts worked, and how they joined
together. It was very awkward. We were standing up. I was trying
to get his penis to go in and kept pushing him closer to me, but
I didn't have the skill set to make it happen. But I knew enough
and I was trying to make it happen. I was very calm. I walked
him through it completely matter of fact. I also recall being very
affectionate and loving. He was a neighbor boy. At the time, I was
living in Memphis with my mom and my stepdad. Looking back
on this, years later, I wonder how I knew any of this? How did I
know how to teach him to have sex?

I don't remember being abused, but there are a few snippets of evidence aside from how I acted toward other children. When I was in my thirties I finally talked to my mom about it. I knew something wasn't right about having so much information about sex as a small child. I asked her if she knew if anything had ever happened to me. I brought it to her by saying, "There's no judgment on you, mom. But obviously, something did happen. I'm just trying to figure it out for myself."

She said, "You know, I left your stepfather for a number of reasons, and there was an incident that was a red flag." At first, I didn't want to believe what she told me next. She said that when I was around five years old, I came into her room and got onto the bed.

I said, "Let's play the game. Let's play the game." She was folding laundry and not really paying attention to me. I laid down and I raised my dress over my head and over my face, exposing myself. She just looked at me.

She said this was the only time there was a red flag. At the time, she didn't connect the dots because she didn't want to process it.

So, she told me, "Put your dress down."

I don't remember this happening, but I know it's true. I can see it in my mind's eye. That's exactly what I would do or say. I remember how I used to come into her room and bounce up on the bed. The memory didn't come back to me, but I knew that what she was saying was true.

Soon after that, we moved away from Memphis. My mom left my stepfather, and we lived in my grandparents' house for a little while. One night, I was staying at my uncle's house and I was sleeping on a pullout bed with the daughter of his girlfriend at the time. She was six and I was maybe eight or nine. She tried to do something sexual with me. I was instantly aware that this was what I had done with the little neighbor boy. At the time, I hadn't given much consideration to what had happened with the neighbor boy but when this little girl initiated with me, I immediately thought, "Oh, no, oh, no, something has happened to her. She's way too young to know to do this. She shouldn't know anything. Why is she trying to touch me in this way?" I didn't know how to handle it, or what to tell her. I wasn't actually that much older than her, but she seemed so young to me.

At the time, I wasn't able to attribute that same line of thinking to myself. I didn't have that lightbulb moment where I realized that something had happened to me when I was little. All I thought was that I had to protect this girl and stop her from continuing to touch me.

I gently pushed her away. I said, "No, we don't do that. Let's just go to sleep. Go sleep on your side of the bed."

She left me alone, and I began to worry. What was I going to say to her mom? What was I going to say to my uncle? What was I going to say to anybody? Because I was so little, I didn't know how to talk about it. I didn't know her mom, and I didn't know what her mom would do. I didn't know what might happen to her relationship with my uncle if I said something. What would happen to this little girl? Would I be in trouble?

I didn't say anything to anyone, but while I was in the house with this little girl I was really watchful. I watched her, and her mother, and my uncle's relationship to this woman. I kept thinking that maybe I should tell my uncle because obviously this girl had something done to her. I thought that this mother was not paying enough attention to notice that something was wrong. I thought that maybe she wasn't a good parent—maybe she wasn't a good person. She wasn't a good mom, and I didn't want my uncle to be involved with someone who wasn't a good mom. Again, I didn't have the ability to extend this thinking to my own experience. I didn't worry about whether or not my own mom should have noticed that something had happened to me. I was just worried for this little girl.

The next incident at my grandparents' house happened when I was around nine or ten. I was caught in a closet with my two boy cousins. One was a year or two older than me and one was a year or two younger. Again, I was the instigator of the sexual contact. I was teaching them. We got caught by my grandparents and we got the tar taken out of us for it.

There was no conversation. My grandmother administered the switch to all of us for it. All she said was, "I never want to see you doing this ever again." At the time, I pretended it wasn't my fault, that the boys instigated it. But it was.

After that I had bouts with my grandparents' next-door neighbors. I had a brush sexual encounter with the older son who was like, seventeen or eighteen. And the father. These were two separate occasions. The encounter with the father happened first. I was somewhere around eight, nine or ten. I think that these incidents all happened at around the same time because at my grandparents' house no one was really watching us that intently.

I was playing outside, and the dad asked me to come into his house. This was their longtime neighbor. There was no reason to be fearful, and I was curious because I had never actually been in their house before. He sat me down on the steps and he gave me a cookie to pacify me. Then he tried to touch me between my legs. I was like, really? You're giving me a cookie to distract me? I didn't think that this was that weird or different because at the time, I was already sexualized. I was mostly focused on how lame it was to think of giving me this cookie. I was like, really? A cookie? Come on, buddy. You can probably do better than this. Like, is this your move? I mean, it is laughable. My second thought, of course, was that he shouldn't be doing this. I shouldn't be allowing him to do this. The third thought was that it was kind of pleasurable, but no, he's not really supposed to be doing this. Eventually I just got up. It was only two minutes or so that I was sitting there with my thoughts eating this cookie. But then I was done with him trying to grope me. It felt weird and stupid, and more than anything I was a little offended. That this was my thought process, in and of itself says a lot.

I was mostly just embarrassed for this old man. He was my grandparents' next door neighbor and he was drunk. I'd never seen him in the state that he was in, so I chalked it up to that. I'd been in his presence before many times and nothing like that had ever happened before, so I just decided he must have been drunk, and I guess horny, and his wife wasn't around. And he had cookies. I rationalized it away because he wasn't really aggressive. Of course, this is through my eyes as a child.

I think this ability of mine to rationalize was fortunate and unfortunate. I had the wherewithal to be more bored by this encounter than anything. This rationalizing also kept me from telling anyone.

I had an encounter with the son of that same neighbor soon after that. It happened at my school. We were in a dark hallway. It was summer, and I don't remember why I was even at the school then. I shouldn't have been. Maybe I was there for summer camp, or maybe he asked me to come to the school with him or maybe he followed me there. He tried to grope me and I was just like, *no* and I just walked away. I was not going to participate in whatever this was. I think the moment he touched me I understood that he could do something more. This was a dark place. No one was around. We weren't even supposed to be in the school. I was also really concerned that this was *my* school. I didn't want this to happen in my school, to be the memory I had of my school. I really respected my school. I felt like, "How dare you? This is my alma mater for the love of God. Shame on you for trying to tarnish my school!" I had lovely childhood years at this place. I had the same sense of boredom I had when his father molested me, but this time there was also a note of fear. I was still around eight or nine. He was a teenage boy, and I think something about this made it feel particularly dangerous. It was the first time I'd ever felt this sort of fear in a sexual situation.

My final childhood sexual encounter was after we moved away from my grandparents' house. I was thirteen. We went on a vacation to Michigan, to a little ranch. I got to ride horses, and it was so amazing.

One of the ranch hands led me away in the barn and he touched my breasts, and it was nauseating to me. That's how I felt it in my body. It sickened me that he touched me in this sexual way. I was having a really positive experience with my family, and he brought something so negative into it. I felt like, "How could you?" All I wanted was to create a memory of this wonderful moment with my family. And then he violated me. That nauseated feeling wasn't really about my body or myself at the time. It was more that now, this was going to be a part of that memory. It could've just been fireflies and horses.

I've never spoken to anyone professionally about any of this. It's always in the back of my mind that I've got to figure out how this is impacting me. How I truly feel about it, how I feel in my body about it, and how it is impacting my relationships. I have spent a lot of time thinking about dealing with this, and how it shows up in my life. I try to be present in that. Very recently I've been trying to do some work on myself around this.

I think what happened to me as a child really impacted my marriages. I went through two of them. I wasn't sexually attracted to either of the people I married. It wasn't the basis for our relationship. I always had this feeling like, sure, we can have sex, but there was no drive for that.

Once those marriages ended, I really began to recognize signs of molestation in my sexual responses. I got into a relationship seven years ago where I was regularly having sex with someone I was attracted to. Looking back on it, although I genuinely wanted the intimacy, I was not really enjoying it. I wasn't being present during sex. It was almost as though I was always just watching myself, like I was critiquing a film.

So I had a discussion with my partner. I said, "I'm going through a thing, and I'm really trying to be present in sex, and I want to talk to you about it. And I want to talk about how we feel and what we want. And I want to be intentional about it, and really enjoy it."

He was way more experienced than me but was closed off emotionally. This wasn't ideal for what I was hoping to accomplish.

I began to notice that I was hiding during sex. Physically, I was feeling pleasure, but mentally I was trying not to. I was shutting down. I think this is a response that came from having been molested, this trying to disconnect from the physical sensation. I was reverting. My response was to hide my face. I would do that involuntarily. I would bring both of my hands up and hide my own face. I kept asking myself, "Why am I doing that? Why am I hiding? Why am I physically hiding? Why am I closing my eyes so tight that my eyelids are flipping over?"

Eventually I thought back to the time I asked my mom to play "the game." How I put my dress over my face. I think that's where I first learned to hide my face when someone was touching me.

I am ready to tell this story, but it is very difficult to get into it and to see how much it has impacted me. I was horrified to see how, as old as I am, this is still affecting my behavior. I feel as though I am my three- or four- or five-year-old self again. I've been trying to repair some of this, and remain in a state of awareness. I'm finally talking about it, and finally talking about it with myself. When I talk to my five-year-old self, I always call her "Five." For years, I've said, "You know, Five, I really don't want to talk to you about this. We have so much to do to keep ourselves together." But I am really trying to make it a point to comfort and take care of that little girl.

I still don't know who molested me, but it is very likely that it was my stepfather. Or that my stepfather allowed someone else in our home who molested me. After I had the conversation with my mom where she mentioned this, I shut down any kind of processing around that and didn't talk to him. I didn't really talk to him anyway, because my mom left him when I was five, but I did have a half sister which kept us connected. I was civil to him.

I still had a degree of love for him. I never spoke to him about it. I didn't trust that he was capable of speaking to me as an adult, even though I was an adult at this time, because in many ways he wasn't one himself. He had an eighth grade education. He came from a very, very poor family, and I'm quite sure there was sexual molestation within that family as well.

It's hard to describe how I feel about him today, because it's still unexplored. I haven't really allowed myself to really feel anything around him. He's dead now. On his deathbed, he reached out to me, and I purposely did not take his call. Maybe if I had, there would have been closure there. But I wasn't ready to talk about it then.

I want to deal with the sadness and the pain around how it's impacted me, but I'm not quite ready to go down that rabbit hole. As far as he's concerned, I don't need him to say anything for me to do better. I don't need him to apologize to me for it to be better. I know that healing is mine to do, so in that way, it doesn't matter to my healing that he has died.

I think it was a gift of mine to be able to rationalize how I did, because it protected me. I wonder, though, if it would have been better at the time to let myself feel. To let myself cry. I think this is what healing looks like for me now. Taking care of the little girl inside me, to let me, and to let her feel. To have a really good cry.

CHAPTER 4

CRYSTAL

"I remember one incident with my little boy cousin.
It was like I wanted to hurt him sexually.
That's the only thing I recall."

I'll be fifty-one in December. Participating in this book feels like kismet. Like I'm ready to talk about this. Like I should tell you everything.

My memory is kind of shaky as far as when was actually the first time my cousin molested me. What I remember is that my parents dropped me off at his house. I think he was fourteen and I was seven. I can kind of recall like it was second or third grade. When I would go over there they would let us stay up late. The whole family would be in the living room watching HBO or Showtime at night. Even then I was conscious that the content of what they were watching wasn't appropriate for me. Some of these shows were borderline softcore porn.

I would sit on the floor with a blanket, in front of the big TV cabinet to watch. Eventually, my cousin, Charlie, came and sat next to me. He would touch me under the blanket. His parents would be on the couch behind us, and I'm still unsure why they didn't see anything, or if they did see something, why they didn't do anything. They had to have known.

The next memory I have is being at his house on a weekend. I don't know why my parents always left me there. I don't know what they were doing or what happened but it would usually be an overnight type of thing. I remember I was walking down the hallway, and my cousin came up from behind me and grabbed me, and picked me up. I struggled and kicked my legs. I was wearing a skirt or short shorts. I remember him putting his finger in between my underwear. Then I remember hearing this weird sound and immense pain. It broke my hymen, but I didn't know that until later. I only realized it in retrospect. I just knew I hurt and there was blood in my underwear but I didn't know what it meant. I wasn't even menstruating yet. I didn't have any context for this experience.

It's so sad to think of myself as that little girl. I've healed enough that I can tell the story of what happened. It's a memory. It's in the past, and I've gotten some healing. Now I'm working on the anger I still hold from it.

I've never spoken to my cousin about this. He's still alive, and if I see him at a wedding or a funeral, he avoids me. I think things might have been different if we actually had gotten the legal system involved. There was a time that it seemed like that might happen. I was fourteen, and had begun going to counseling and talking about it. But then I ran away from home and that started a lot of trouble, because running away was illegal. Then, they noticed all the cuts on my arm. I ended up in a lockdown facility for kids and was there for around two weeks. When my dad got the bill for my time at the facility, he was livid. It was about $5,000. He was so mad he didn't want me to come back home. I had to go into foster care for a day or two. Then I went to live with my aunt, the mother of the cousin who abused me.

Because of my cousin's abuse, I did act out sexually as a child in a few small ways. I remember one incident where I did something to my little boy cousin. He was probably three and I was eight. I don't remember what it was exactly, but I remember being embarrassed about doing it. It was like I wanted to hurt him sexually. That's the only thing I recall. Otherwise, it was always some other little kid doing something to me first. I had another cousin that did stuff to me, but he was my age. I think because of this, it seemed safer. It was more like mutual experimentation. He was from the same side of the family but was the son of a different aunt. I was around nine when this started, so I was already a couple years into being molested by Charlie. I also ended up experimenting with girls later in my adolescence. I think it was because there was something safer to being with girls after what Charlie had done to me. This ended up confusing me at the time. I grew up in the church and it was considered ungodly to be gay. But I also had all kinds of gay people on my mom's side of the family, and they weren't evil or bad or anything. I was with girls when I was a girl, and I wasn't evil either. I was also so afraid of men, so afraid of penises because of what my cousin had done to me. I entered adulthood very confused. Since then, I've had long relationships with both men and women. I think I'm more interested in a spiritual connection than I am in a particular gender. I now consider my attraction to be spiritual, and myself to be gender fluid.

I was around eleven when my older cousin stopped molesting me. The abuse had developed from groping to him attempting to penetrate me. We'd be playing Monopoly or something, and eventually my sister and my other cousins would get tired and go to bed. He would coerce me to stay in the room with him. He would shut the door to keep me there. I was scared of him. He was twice my size, height-wise, but probably three or four times my weight. Or if I did start to sleep without him having done anything, I'd wake up to him on top of me and trying to penetrate me.

The last time he tried anything, I was at his house one Saturday and he had a friend over. And I remember him saying something like, "Watch this." As he picked me up, he started fumbling around. I was more frightened than I'd ever been, because I was scared of what the two of them might do. So I started fighting. I started kicking and screaming until he let go. I ran out the back door and I slammed the sliding glass door and just glared at him from behind the glass. Then I ran to where my aunt was, to safety. That was the last time he tried to molest me. He stopped coming into my room at night when I would stay over. But I still have issues sleeping. Certain songs from the '70s freak me out and trigger me. I've struggled with starving myself and then with overeating because I think a part of me thought that if I gained weight I would be less sexually attractive and these experiences of abuse might stop.

My healing process has been a long one, but I have gained so much peace. A major change for me was learning how to meditate. I would also ask for Spirit to show me my memories in my dreams. I always ask to be shown in a gentle way so I am able to deal with what happened. I say this with caution. I would approach trying to remember what happened in a way that still feels safe, but Spirit will show you what you need to see in order to heal.

Eventually, I was able to let Charlie go. I actually had a vision of myself hugging him, and looking into his eyes. I saw him as a little kid getting molested by somebody.

Once I revisited what happened and processed it, Spirit told me not to hold on to memories. Not those memories, and not even good memories. It is best to live in the present. Sometimes taking out pleasant memories and looking at them, perhaps with loved ones, can be nice. But generally, I don't go back to things, and I don't go into the future. I just stay in the present. I've become very spiritual. I meditate a lot and set intentions. I work with lucid dreaming and astral projection. Through this, I've learned that I am a healer. I heal myself and others through Reiki and toroidal fields—the energetic aura of the body. I help people release their trauma from that energetic field so that it doesn't become disease. We go into the past so that we can let the past go.

You have to have self love to start healing. You have to have compassion for yourself, the child you were, and the inner child that still lives inside you. You have to forgive yourself. Have somebody help you, a counselor, someone from your spiritual path, even a higher power or your higher self. Take responsibility for your healing by giving yourself that love and compassion. For anyone on this path, I hold a bubble of protection around them while they are healing. I hold an image of wholeness, and of fullness. All of us are capable of healing. All of us are capable of walking around in wholeness. And wouldn't that be just spectacular, all of us healed and fulfilled and whole?

If you need help healing, please click or scan this QR Code to access my resources page.

Resource Center at www.jilleschultz.com/gethelp

Or turn to the Resource Center on page 179 to get help.

PART 2

I FOUND FORGIVENESS

*"As you process your sexual trauma,
I do not ask that you forget but for your sake,*

*I hope that you can start to forgive.
Whoever hurt you was most likely hurt by someone else.*

Hurt people, hurt people."

—*My prayer for you*

CHAPTER 5

RODNEY

"I realized at this point, I could actually do something about it now. I could hurt him if I wanted to."

I am forty-six, and I've been telling my story for a long time. It means a lot to me to tell my story because it helps the people I serve. I think it also helps that other men see me, an African-American man, share my story. I want other ethnic males to understand that it is okay to be open about their trauma. If something like this happened to them, it's okay, and it's healing to talk about it.

I'm originally from Des Moines, Iowa. Born and raised. I don't know how we got to Iowa, but we got there. I grew up in a little community. It's the southeast side of the city. I still have family there. My mom and dad still live there. Nobody ever seems to leave.

There's a rec center there that used to be an old school. A lot of my family members went to the school when they were kids, but by the time I was coming up it had been turned into the center. I believe the city basically took it over and senior citizens mostly used it during the day. In the evenings, once the kids got out of school, they got to use it. It was pretty influential for the community. It kept a lot of kids off the street, and kept a lot of kids safe. But ironically enough, that's where the abuse happened to me. I was around seven or eight years old. I put all of this away for so long that I have even questioned it if it really happened. But I know it happened.

I had a core group at the rec center. My friends, my brother and his friends. We all grew up together. But we pretty much knew everyone at the center, they were all either from the neighborhood of a nearby school. My brother was ten years older than me, and he had this casual friend. He and this guy weren't that close and I always thought he was always a little weird.

He started showing up when my older brother was gone doing something else. I am sure he waited until my brother, who was very protective of me, wasn't around. Sometimes I wonder how much he planned it, but I'm assuming he was probably a predator. He probably knew what he was doing. He was around seventeen or eighteen.

It would happen in the rec center bathroom. There were adults supervising, but it was sometimes like twenty kids to one adult. Sometimes the adults were around and sometimes they wouldn't be. It was the perfect opportunity. The bathroom was down a hall, and there were about four stalls. The actual physicality of the abuse gets fuzzy for me. I know there was oral sex. I know it happened several times. I know there was bribery, too. They had candy machines and he would give me candy so that I would keep what had happened to myself. The center was just across the street from my house. I remember in the wintertime he would actually walk me to my house to take me home so my family knew him, and trusted him to some degree. I know the abuse happened more than three or four times. Then, eventually, it stopped. I don't know why it stopped or how it stopped.

I didn't tell my story to my mother until I was about nineteen. I was home on a break from college. My mom was watching Oprah Winfrey. She loved Oprah Winfrey, I mean, who doesn't? But in this episode the topic was child molestation. It went to a commercial. I looked at my mom and I went, "Mom, I want to let you know something. I was molested."

She was gone! I mean, she was sitting there, but it was like her soul left her. And then she started crying. She wanted to know who, and I tried not to tell her but eventually I did. She was in shock. She asked, "Why didn't you tell me?"

I said, "I was a kid. I didn't even think to tell anyone—and he told me not to tell." The reality of it is, as a kid, if you don't tell anyone, you don't even know how bad what's happening might be. You don't know if it's normal, or bad, or good. All you know is that something is happening. It takes someone telling you that it is bad to really realize it. I explained this to her and she just cried and cried. My dad was at work, but eventually he came home. So he comes walking through the door and sees mom crying.

And so I told my dad, "Dad, I just told mom that I was sexually molested as a kid."

He said, "What! When?" I told him it was when I was eight or nine. He looked up at a china cabinet we had that was filled with pictures. There was one picture of me in there when I was around that same age. He looked at it and said, "That's when you were being sexually molested?" And I shook my head. I didn't know what to say. "You were such a happy kid," he said, and then he paused. "If you would have told me this when you were a kid, I would have killed him."

I said, "Yeah, I know." I realize now that that is probably partly why I didn't tell him. It kept me from saying anything. What, I was going to tell, and then my dad would do something, and I'd grow up without a dad?

My brother said the same thing, too, when I called him later that day and told him. He would have killed him, too. He had so much guilt for not being able to have protected me. That was a tough day.

Later that same year, around New Year's, I was at a dance club in Des Moines with a couple of friends. I remember going to the bar and getting a drink or some water or something. I turned around, and I saw the guy who had molested me across the club. I recognized his face. I was a chubby kid growing up, but by this time I was playing college football, so I did nothing but lift, eat and study. I was a pretty big guy. And I had a decision to make.

I realized at this point, I could actually do something about it now. I could hurt him if I wanted to. I stood there and processed what I wanted to do. I remember observing my emotions, processing my options. And then I decided not to take action.

He eventually came up to me and tried to make small talk. I was respectful because by this time, I had already forgiven him. I didn't bring it up. I didn't mention it. I made the conversation short. I ended it with something like, "Have a good New Year, bye." And I walked away. That was the last time I saw him in person.

In my healing process, I didn't end up going to therapy or anything like that. I really believe it was more of doing work within myself. It wasn't formal work. When it came to him, I realized that it wasn't my fault. Even at a very young age, I realized that that wasn't my fault. As a kid people always told me I was an old soul. I've always been a thinker. Through this I realized that I haven't always been trusting with people, probably because of what happened to me. I figured out that in order for me to move on with my life, I would need to forgive him for what he did. It sounds simple, but I think that was really what helped. I made peace with myself at a young age and I proclaimed it as done and now I get to share my story and help others to move on. That is why I wanted to be part of this book. I really want to help people to forgive and heal.

I don't feel compassion for him, but I don't feel hate. It is freeing to have forgiven him in a way where I don't feel anything about him at all.

I started talking openly about what happened to me soon after I told my parents. At one point in college, I was studying social work and I had to do a presentation. I ended up choosing the subject for the presentation out of a hat and ironically or NOT, the topic was sexual abuse. I couldn't figure out how I wanted to start it. Eventually, I ended up by saying, "Envision a kid running around, with a lot of energy because he has a learning disability. He's got a lot of things working against him, including being sexually molested. So imagine that kid. Actually, the kid is standing in front of you today. I was sexually molested." Then I went on to the rest of my presentation. So I didn't hide it. I think that had a lot to do with nobody knowing until I was an adult. I didn't feel shame around it because when it was happening I was too young to understand that it was shameful, and when I told people about it as an adult they were supportive. I've always been kind of at peace sharing my story. There are so many people out there going through the same thing.

Sharing my story has also helped me empathize with the people I serve. I'm a social worker, and I'm working on my master's degree. I am a life coach as well. I've always been upfront about what happened to me. It sometimes helps to build that connection, especially when so many people have experienced something similar.

It took me a while to realize that there was a difference between sharing my story and being truly emotionally open. In my earlier relationships, the women I dated would tell me that they couldn't really tell how I was feeling. In my mind, I'm thinking, "I am sharing my feelings!" But the reality is I was keeping a part of myself protected. I've always been the type of man to cry at movies, and I don't perceive myself as being macho. But even my wife said that early on in our marriage I was a little harder to reach. I was more reserved. Now she says I'm much more open with my feelings. She's helped me get there. And it's really helped me help other people who have lived through the same thing.

Resource Center at www.jilleschultz.com/gethelp
Or turn to the Resource Center on page 179 to get help.

CHAPTER 6

NICOLE

*"So many of us block what has happened to us,
and when we remember, that shadow can
feel all-encompassing. But what happened to you isn't who
you are. That shadow isn't who you are.
Who you are is light."*

'm fifty-seven. I want to start by saying how grateful I am to be a part of this book, and that this book is going to be out in the world. Having gone through so much of my own therapy, I finally realize that what I experienced isn't that uncommon. But it's not being spoken about. I think that speaking about this is part of putting the shame away and also walking back into forgiveness on all levels. When we're children, we do what we learn. We don't know to do anything differently. We do what we're taught even if it is wrong, because we don't know that it's wrong. We may know that something is wrong somewhere deep inside, but we can't quite identify it.

I'm a big open book when it comes to talking about my experiences because I've been processing it for so long. My story, in a nutshell, is that I was actually sexually abused starting at about eighteen months old, though my first memory of the abuse is from when I was around three. Almost all of the men in my childhood sexually abused me, from my uncle, to a stepfather, to a school teacher to a neighbor. Because of my history of abuse, I drew in relationships that were less than perfect. I've been raped three times as an adult, by people I trusted.

I began my therapy when I was in my twenties and it was very helpful. Because I had begun to process, I thought I was very okay with my sexuality and never opened up to my first husband about the abuse. That marriage was also unsafe, so of course I didn't open up. During my second marriage, I did tell my husband about the abuse. He later used this information against me. He eventually left me, right after I'd gotten into a car accident.

Because the experience of opening up and then having my story weaponized was so violating, I haven't been intimate with anyone for seven years now.

This has given me time to focus on choosing to fully heal myself. My whole self. I'm walking through what it is like truly loving myself. I'm processing a sort of encompassing abuse—both my childhood sexual abuse and the abuse I drew into my adult life due to the things I'd learned as a child.

I don't remember acting out sexually with other children. When I was seven or eight I remember playing doctor, and there seemed to be some opportunity for experimentation, but I didn't go through with it. While it is common for children who are being abused to be promiscuous, I wasn't. I had this desire to be "pure." This obviously came from the feelings of impurity and shame from having been abused by a family member. My uncle hurt me from the time I was eighteen months old. It took me until I was around thirteen or fourteen to stand up to him and say, "No more."

I think part of the reason he abused me is because he wasn't taught not to. He was treated like a child by my family, even once he'd become an adult. He'd been in two car accidents, and to my knowledge, he had always lived with my grandmother. He was not right and functioned as an adolescent. He was the only one out of five who never left their house. My mom was very close with her parents, so we lived on the property as well, which made me easy to access. My mom had four children prior to meeting my dad, but they didn't live with us. I know my older sisters were also abused by my uncle, though not as consistently. But it only takes once to potentially ruin a life. My oldest sister ended up drinking herself to death.

Years later, I was working with a Native American shaman and was speaking with him about forgiveness. I realized that because of the time and because of the family dynamic, everything that my uncle was doing was shoved under the rug. The family pretended it wasn't happening. Because my uncle still had the functioning of an adolescent even in his adulthood, he needed to be taught explicitly what was right and what was wrong, and nobody taught him that.

He had access to a lot of *Playboy* magazines. I don't know if someone gave them to him or if he got them himself but I really believe that he saw those images and he wanted to replicate what was happening in those magazines. He had access to me and I looked like the girls in his magazines, so that's what I was, the girls in the magazines. Not really *real*. I was like a doll to him. Because the idea of sexual abuse was so unspeakable, so hidden, no one ever taught him not to do what he was doing. I don't think he was ever sexually abused himself, I just think that he got stuck in an age where he didn't have a certain self control or understanding and no one intervened to properly guide him. By seeing him this way, I was able to forgive him.

In some ways, forgiveness comes easy to me because I have such a degree of love for humanity and for people in general. I see everything as a piece of or an extension of me. When I think of my uncle, I really understand the devastation of his life. He was incredibly tormented. Eventually, he died in a suicide by cop. He barricaded himself into the house and I believe there was someone in there with him. He may have been holding that person hostage. I'm really not sure of the details, because at that point I hadn't had any contact with him for a very long time. Someone left me a message explaining what had happened. Eventually, the police got him to come out of the house, but he had a gun. Apparently, he wasn't being aggressive with it, but because he had the gun, the cops had no other choice but to shoot him. I feel it is possible he did this on purpose.

I've never counted the total number of men who molested me, but there are at least ten. My uncle, my stepfather, my neighbor, school teachers, boyfriends, a husband, a guy that did my hair, a guy I worked with, a guy who raped me.

I believe I was targeted by this many people because my circumstances made me vulnerable. My uncle had such easy access to me, and even though he was abusing me, I remained so trusting. For example, the neighbor who molested me would often walk around his house in his underwear when I went to go play with his kids. I didn't really think anything about it. It was the early '70s and it seemed like kind of a normal thing, maybe, or at least normal within their family. When I would stay the night and have a sleepover with his daughters, he would sneak into the bedroom and fondle me. As I got to be an adult, I realized he had to have been doing that to his girls as well. He had two little girls.

But here's how trusting I was. I knew it didn't feel right, but I also didn't know how wrong it was. One day he said to me, "Do you want to learn even more about this and do you want to know where babies come from?" At that time, baby dolls were a big thing for me. I was a little girl. I loved baby dolls and I loved babies. I had no idea what he really meant, but I remember thinking, "Oh my gosh, yes, I can't wait to learn about where babies come from." Some time later I said to a babysitter of mine, "I gotta go over to Mr. Boardman's house because he's going to show me where babies come from." Even though he was molesting me, I was still so excited by this idea and so trusting that I wanted to go.

I don't fully remember what happened but I'm sure the babysitter didn't let me go because I never saw him again. The next thing I knew was someone told me that they'd moved to New York. Maybe the cops went over. I don't really know what transpired because back in those days everything was shoved under the rug nothing was talked about. But I assume something happened because they disappeared.

Not only was I easy to access and trusting, but I also think that, in a messed up way, the way Mr. Boardman was treating me made me feel special. My dad had left and even though he already had two little girls, he was singling me out for attention; even though it was abusive, it made me feel like, "Oh, I must be something very special." Even though it wasn't comfortable, in fact it was very uncomfortable, still the fact that I was receiving a lot of attention felt good.

When I was sexually abused by a teacher, I know that this certainly did not have the same effect. It did not make me feel special. It felt very very dirty. Back in those days, when they would show videos in the classrooms they would make the room very dark. I don't know if he did this to other girls, but sometimes during the videos he would make me sit on his lap and he would fondle me in the dark. I remember withdrawing more and more, and feeling deep shame.

These early experiences made me susceptible to later abuse. They made abuse feel normal. I've been married twice. My first husband was very abusive, and he raped me the night before I left. Getting out of this relationship actually ended up helping me reconnect with my dad and I moved to another state to be with him. This was the first time I'd seen or talked to him since he left when I was five. Once I moved in with my dad, we started having conversations about the sexual abuse. It's actually my dad who shared with me that he believes the abuse started when I was eighteen months old. When I was eighteen months old, my uncle brought me in from the desert, naked and crying. He told my family that I had wandered off, and that he had rescued me. No one thought anything about it at the time. My family assumed that I'd been crying because I'd gotten lost. I don't think it crossed their minds that he had hurt me. During my healing process, I was eventually able to access this memory. I was terrified, confused and had no voice, being that I was so little. I became confused because the person who had taken me and hurt me was now being glorified and told how great he was for saving me. This really clarified my sense of confusion in regards to the role of adults in my early life. My natural understanding was that adults would keep me safe and protect me, even though in actuality, they didn't.

Talking to my dad about the abuse finally made me understand why my first solid memory of the abuse was when I was around three. My dad actually walked in on my uncle molesting me and hurting me when I was three, which I think is why I have such a strong memory of abuse at that age.

The family did nothing to keep my uncle away from me. Eventually, I asked my dad, "Why did you leave me in that?" And he told me he just didn't know what to do. So it was just shoved under the rug. When we did reconnect I was twenty-five, and from there my dad and I were able to actually build a beautiful relationship, because we were able to be honest about everything.

When I was thirteen or fourteen, I spoke up about my uncle's abuse. My grandmother basically disowned me.

I don't recall my mother's initial reaction. Later, when I would share openly, she didn't know what to do with her shame and guilt. My mom was great. She had such a beautiful soul, and she loved me deeply.

I don't recall being sexually active as a teen. I did have a boyfriend, and I got pregnant at fourteen, and I ended up having an abortion all on my own. Of course I must have been sexually active because I became pregnant, but I have no memory of it. I would guess that it is due to trauma. Nobody knew about my pregnancy or my abortion. I was devastated. It was the hardest thing I'd ever done in my life, because it was almost like I was split into two people. One part of me knew about the sexual world and my body. But a bigger part of me was still very naive and very innocent. I think if I hadn't had so much shame, and if I'd had someone to talk to about these things, some of my relationships would have been different. But I kept things hidden, and stuffed what had happened to me down inside myself.

After my first marriage, after building all this trust with my dad and doing so much healing, I ended up in another relationship where sex was being used as a means of control. I had walked away from my first relationship and done enough work that I really loved and enjoyed sex. With my second husband, I thought I had been very discerning in my choices in my relationships. Once we got married, however, he would withhold sex and attention to control me. He would go months without touching me and make me feel dirty for the things I wanted. The last time we had sex he made me feel truly awful, saying that I disgusted him. When he finally left, I knew he had been with other women, even though we were still married. It was very in my face, he may have even brought some of them into our home when I wasn't present. This really triggered the feelings of shame and unworthiness that started early in my childhood. I had to begin healing all over again. I am continuing to prioritize and commit to my healing before I enter another relationship.

I have done so much work over the years. I never really used substances or outside sources to deal with the pain and shame of all the sexual abuse, but when I was in my teens I did end up with a pretty severe eating disorder. This went on for about fourteen or fifteen years. At one point I ended up weighing only eighty-eight pounds. Everyone thought that I developed this disorder because I was trying to be thin, but it was actually because I was stuffing down all the shame, hurt, abandonment and guilt that I had no idea I was still carrying. I thought that because I could speak openly about my abuse and didn't have an issue with being intimate that I was healed. It is clear to me now that the eating disorder came from a need to be witnessed in my pain. In my thirties I started a different type of therapy that was directed at sexual abuse and found that once I started to feel heard, look within and forgive, the need to restrict food was gone. Thank God I was able to overcome this, but my healing work is still ongoing. I'm not currently in an intimate relationship, but now it is my choice not to be intimate. I'm waiting until I've had enough time with myself to continue to work through this.

For me, the first step has always been forgiveness. I start by stepping out of myself and putting myself in the shoes of those who hurt me. I know that they wouldn't have abused me if something bad hadn't happened to them. But still, when I imagine myself in their shoes, I make a different choice than they did. I don't hurt the little me. These last seven years have been about forgiving and loving myself.

I think forgiveness is a gift that we give, so that we can evolve. We can let go, and grow, and change, and get better. I think this book is so powerful because we can all learn from each other's stories. So many of us are so far removed from the sacredness of who we are. We forget our true nature, and think our lives happen outside of ourselves instead of going inward. We think it's all happening out there instead of looking in. I was alone so much as a child, and I spent so much time outside, that through nature I was able to connect with God. I wasn't raised religiously. I didn't know at the time that this connection was God and Jesus showing up in my life, but it was. I realize now that I was never truly alone, even though I spent years feeling this way. This relationship with my creative Source, that I call God, has shown me all the areas within myself that I still needed to uncover, to feel, and to forgive in order to heal.

I think of this book as a catalyst to help people remember not just what happened to them, but also who they truly are. So many of us block what has happened to us, and when we remember, that shadow can feel all-encompassing. But what happened to you isn't who you are. That shadow isn't who you are. Who you are is light.

CHAPTER 7

SCOTT

"At the end of the day, he was nine and so was I.
Forgiving Bobby let me forgive myself.
Neither of us were abusers. We were nine-year-old boys."

I'm fifty-seven. As a child, I thought I was growing up in a perfect family. Now I realize that I was neglected. I wasn't really wanted. It was very well known that I was a mistake. I really struggled to relate to my brother and my dad. My dad would tell me that I was too sensitive. That I should have been a girl. That they should have called me Suzie instead of Scott. I was nine years old when we moved to a new house in a new state. I had no friends, and did not feel safe in my home.

I feel like this might have made me an easy target, or at the very least susceptible to anyone who might show me some attention. Any male that would show me attention. It might have happened anyway. It certainly could have happened if I had had a safe home and strong bonds with my family. But I think my home life was part of the recipe for what happened. I was just looking for someone to connect with.

I started to make some friends in our new neighborhood. The first person I met was a girl who lived next door. We got along great. We were great friends. But I was still looking for a boy to connect with. Eventually I met Bobby. He lived in a house behind us, and we started hanging out. He was an only child, and he lived in a bigger house than ours. He invited me to spend the night at his house. It starts to get a little blurry here. I am pretty sure it was the first night I stayed over. I can't remember how long I'd known him at this point. But this all happened fairly soon after we moved to the area.

We probably played outside for a bit and had dinner. At some point his mom told us it was time to go to bed. We went to his room, and I was a little surprised to see that he only had one bed and she hadn't set up a place for me to sleep on the floor or anything. I remember that the bed was small, at most it was a double but more likely it was a twin.

He had a television in his room, which was exciting because I didn't have one in mine. We watched movies for a while. At some point he asked me, "Do you want to pretend like we're married?" I had no idea what he meant by this. I said no. I just wanted to watch whatever movie or show we were watching. He asked two or three more times in different ways, such as, "Why don't we? It'd be fun. I've done it before." I wasn't really disturbed by it, but I wasn't interested in it either.

I repeatedly said "No thanks, I'm good."

Eventually he was like, "Come on, why don't you just try for fun? Why don't you get on top of me?" And he told me to take my clothes off. I think I just had a t-shirt and shorts on and underwear. I took off my shirt and my shorts. He had taken off all his clothes.

And then he said, "Take off the underwear, too." And I did. And I was on top of him. I don't remember moving that much. I think he was moving, though.

At some point in time, his mom opened the door. I'm still very curious about this. We were under the covers, but I think it was kind of obvious that something was going on. She said, "You guys are being loud. Gotta keep it down." Then she left, and I remember being surprised because I felt like she had to know what we were doing. I felt like we were doing something wrong, and it seemed like she didn't think we were. And Bobby didn't think we were doing anything wrong, either. Or maybe she just didn't know.

Even though it felt wrong, I liked Bobby. Bobby gave me attention. Bobby wanted to be with me. He was another boy my age in the neighborhood. And physically, it felt good.

There was one other incident, but it wasn't the same. He asked if I wanted to spend the night again. And honestly, I did. I had a good night the last time. I had a good overall experience being there. I can't explain it. I enjoyed being at their house, his parents were nice. They made dinner just for us. It was very interesting for me to be in that house because I had three older brothers and sisters. It was just him and his parents. And I was his friend, and when I was there they made me feel special. They spent all this time and attention talking to me. I don't feel like anybody ever did that. They even asked me what I liked to eat and gave me something different than what he had. Like they prepared a special meal just for me.

His dad had a really nice car. He had a lot of nice toys. I thought that pretending to be married was weird, but overall, I was happy to have spent the night with them. I think it's important to note that and I thought Bobby was a cool kid.

The next time I spent the night we actually went to stay at his grandparents house. His Mom drove me and Bobby over there. In my nine-year-old brain, it felt like it was out in the country a little bit. The house was older and didn't have any other houses around it. We stayed up watching TV in their family room. I believe they put sleeping bags down. I remember watching a boxing match. His grandparents had gone to bed. We were in front of the television and Bobby said, "Hey, you wanna do something fun?"

I said, "Like what?"

And then he said, "You're gonna really like this. It's a lot of fun. I grab my dick and I hold it. And if I hold it for a long time, it feels really good. I'll show you how. You grab my dick, and I'll grab yours." And so he grabbed my dick. And he asked me to grab his. And he said, "Squeeze it harder, squeeze harder, harder." And he did the same to mine, until all of a sudden it started throbbing and then it felt wonderful. I had my first orgasm. It was dry, as I hadn't hit puberty. It was the most amazing feeling I'd ever felt. It was confusing and bewildering and fun and exciting and strange. I felt like I did something wrong, but I enjoyed it.

Because I didn't understand it, I thought maybe this was something that all boys knew about, and maybe I was the only one that didn't know. As much as a part of me felt it was wrong, a part of me felt that it was right. And I felt closer to Bobby. I had a bond with him that I didn't have with anyone else. I liked him. I thought he was a great guy.

This, coupled with the way my dad and brother treated me, ended up really making me question my sexuality. They always made fun of me for being sensitive, and it made me so worried that I was gay. Now I know that there are gay guys who are sensitive and there are gay guys who aren't, and straight guys who are sensitive and straight guys who aren't. I'm a straight guy who is sensitive. But it really confused me for a while. It also stopped me from telling anyone about what had happened with Bobby. I was already so frightened of being seen as gay that I knew my dad and brother could never find out.

It took me a while to forgive myself for spending the night there a second time. Why would I spend the night there again? Because it felt good. But for years, I could forgive myself for the first time because I didn't know it was going to happen. It was the second time that I really struggled with.

Eventually I started making friends with other guys in the neighborhood. I don't really remember how it happened, but we slowly grew apart. I think as I made other guy friends, I felt less lonely. I mean, I still saw him around the neighborhood. I don't remember spending the night with him again. But it's not like I decided I couldn't be with him. At the same time, I think there was something inside me that knew it would be healthier not to be around him.

I didn't tell anyone this until six years ago. I just carried it around with me forever and hid it from the people I tell everything else to. If I told anyone, I thought it would lead people to start asking questions. Like, why didn't you do something to stop it? Why didn't you tell anyone? You must have wanted it. Are you gay? What's your problem?

Six years ago, my therapist helped walk me through it. I had become severely burnt out, which ended up being one of the most beautiful gifts in the world, because it brought me to recovery. And recovery brought me to really pull back the layers and grapple with things I was avoiding forever. I had thought that going back into the past was pointless, but then I realized it was affecting me in the present. I started healing so many old wounds. Like, what it was like to grow up in my home not being wanted. Being told that my mom had a nervous breakdown after I was born. That I was a mistake. And then, there was that secret I had.

My therapist was so helpful. I was so frightened to share this that I almost thought he was going to kick me out of the office. I thought I was as guilty as Bobby in this situation, that we had both participated in something bad. But surprisingly enough, my therapist did not kick me out of his office when I opened up about it. Instead, he told me that he'd seen situations like this many times. We slowly walked through who had responsibility in the situation. Did I want it ahead of time? No. Did I know it was going to happen the first time? No. If I had, would I have still gone over the house? Probably not.

Even still, it doesn't neatly fit into a category. I've come to a beautiful conclusion that yes, the situation was abuse. But I don't see Bobby as an abuser. There doesn't have to be an abuser for there to have been abuse.

Now I wonder, what must have happened to Bobby? Something must have happened to him. He had to learn that somehow. He learned the things he taught me from someone else, I believe. I have a deep curiosity around this, and deep forgiveness for him. At the end of the day, he was nine and so was I. Forgiving Bobby let me forgive myself. Neither of us were abusers. We were nine-year-old boys.

I am so grateful for my therapist's guidance through this. What's crazy is that he is an expert in sexual trauma and sexual addiction, but that isn't why I went to him. I just went because I was experiencing burnout. His expertise ended up being such a gift. I know that it wasn't a coincidence. Every time I would go in to talk to him, I knew I had something to say but I was so scared to say it. And each session always ended up being the most beautiful experience for me. I hope anyone with a similar experience to mine will go talk to somebody. Being able to work up to saying it, to chip away at my layers, helped me finally speak about what happened. Speaking about it began to normalize it. And that's a powerful thing. Not that what happened to me *should* normally happen, but it does happen. It happens to lots of people. It is such a release to know you're not alone. It felt like huge backpacks of boulders being taken off my back when I was finally able to open up about it.

One time, in a session, my therapist asked me, "Why do you think God made you to be a sensitive man?" And it was a turning point in my entire life. I broke down crying, but not out of sadness. It's hard to even explain the emotion. It was everything mixed in at once. It was painful, but I was so overwhelmingly grateful to release all of the pain that this had caused me. To let the pain go. It's really beautiful. What happened to me is part of who I am. It can actually be beautiful, because I am beautiful, if that makes sense. I am happy to be who I am now. And if it hadn't happened just the way it had, if it was an adult, I would have to struggle with feelings of blame. If it had been a female person, I wouldn't have had to ask those questions about my sexuality. And I'm glad I asked those questions. I'm glad I am sensitive. It's made me who I am.

My wife reminds me all the time that she loves how sensitive I am, and when I finally shared all of this with her, all the things I'd been afraid of happening didn't happen. She didn't think about running. Instead, she helped me explore what this sensitivity meant to me. She hadn't realized how deep my sensitivity went. She told me that she never really saw me that way, because I'd learned to try to hide that piece of me. She responded with such gentleness and curiosity. Now she sees this sensitivity in me all the time. It's become a beautiful part of our relationship.

This burden gets lighter and lighter every time I share my story, because now I share it to help others. I'm a sponsor in a Christ-centered addiction recovery program called Celebrate Recovery. It's for all types of addictions. More than two-thirds of the people that come have addictions that aren't chemical. It's people who are addicted to sex. They're addicted to social media. They're addicted to work, they're addicted to codependency, or TV.

If you are seeking help, click or scan this QR Code to view the Resource Center page at my website.

—*Jill E. Schultz*

Resource Center at www.jilleschultz.com/gethelp

Or turn to the Resource Center on page 179 to get help.

My first recognized addiction is that I am a workaholic. It came from my feeling that I had to earn love. I've let go of all of that, but I still give back to the program as a leader and a sponsor. And every time I share my story someone ends up coming up to me and saying, "Thank you. Something like that happened to me too."

I have found so much healing, and I wish that for Bobby, too. I come across him occasionally on things like LinkedIn. He's the CEO of a big company now. When I see his profile, or think of him, I just think, gosh, I hope he has found peace. I hope he's been able to share his story. I hope he's been able to release it. If I saw him now I would say, "Man, I release you from it. And I hope you have found healing like I have." Maybe I'll write him a letter someday and say exactly that.

Having carried this burden for so long and then finally experiencing the joy of releasing it creates in me such a strong urge and desire to help somebody release it today. Wherever and whoever they are. This is why I share my story. This is why I feel called to speak about this. I see you. You are not alone. Healing truly is possible.

CHAPTER 8

CLAIRE

"The first time I was molested I was about two and a half. It was my brother and his friend. They were fifteen and sixteen, and they were drunk. There was penetration and I had to be taken to the hospital."

I'm fifty-nine. When I hit fifty, I realized how much I had shoved everything down. For my whole life, I had coped by not feeling anything. It's interesting to consider how common it is to feel shame around these sorts of experiences. At the time, I felt no shame because I felt nothing. I didn't do feelings. If a feeling did burble up, I tried to control it. I was very, very, very good at shoving things down until it got to a point where I was like a dormant volcano. Everything was quiet on the surface, but there was the magma underneath. When I turned fifty it exploded.

It was triggered by something that seemed so unrelated at first. I got some blood work done and my triglycerides were high, like off the charts high. That was the first time I'd really thought about death. Any moment, I could have a stroke or a heart attack and leave my husband and my sons. Then I lost my job. It was one of those combination "You're fired"/"I quit" type of things. My dad had just died about a month before that. Then, a week later, my father-in-law died. I dealt with the estate on my side, my husband dealt with the estate on his side. All of a sudden, we had all of this to deal with—death, job loss, health scare, and both of our fathers' houses.

Then, suddenly, I had time to take a break. The estates had left us with a little money, and I didn't have a job. For the first time in fifty years, I had a chance to look at who I was and what I wanted to do going forward.

Throughout my life, I was never happy no matter what. I knew I had a lot of pain inside me, but I didn't want to address that pain. It took this calm after the storm for me to begin to address it. I began meditation and yoga. I tried every different modality I could find. I became interested in crystals and in dimensional shifts. Even as I began this journey, I was still avoiding deep processing. I was actually proud of the fact that nobody could crack me.

I got married and became pregnant very young. I went to college when my son was a baby. I excelled in college and began this very heavy job where it was all men. Of course, I had to be better in order to be taken seriously. This intensity came somewhat naturally to me, because from the time I was born, my life was about survival. This was me moving from one survival mindset to another. The first, surviving all of the physical, sexual and emotional abuse in my family. Then, moving into survival again, for me and my family, our future, etc. This is how I was able to make it to fifty without even having taken time to think for myself. This was how I was able to push down all of that pain.

The first time I was molested I was about two and a half. It was my brother and his friend. They were fifteen and sixteen, and they were drunk. There was penetration and I had to be taken to the hospital.

This set the tone for a childhood in which I was continually molested. After that, it just seemed natural. In our family, it seemed like molesting people or being molested was the thing to do, and that's all anyone ever wanted. It was the only connection you could have with somebody. That's what I had learned.

I am still not sure how my mom covered up what happened to me when I was two. I can remember coming to. There was a nurse there with a popsicle, and my mom was standing in the doorway and would not come into the room. My mom and I have a complicated relationship. I moved out when I was twelve. That kind of gives you an idea of how hard things were.

She was very aware of what had happened with my brother. She knew what happened, but she covered it up until she died. I can still remember that she wouldn't come into the room, and I remember the look on her face. I don't even know how to describe it. It was a combination of fear, hatred, disgust, shame, and regret. She couldn't even come into the room, much less calm me and take care of me.

I was told I had had my tonsils removed. That's why I was in the hospital. When I was in kindergarten, though, I missed half the school year because I had strep throat so badly. You're really not supposed to get strep throat once your tonsils have been removed. Then, much later, when I was about twenty-six, I got strep throat really, really badly. I went to the doctor. He looked into my mouth and said, "Well, your tonsils are really enlarged." I said, "But I don't have any tonsils."

That's how much I had shoved it down.

My brother continued to molest me until I was about six or seven. Then he got married and moved away. I think it would have continued if he'd stayed in the home.

Before my mother passed away, she made me the executor of her will. The way it was written was to split the money equally between me, the older brother who had molested me, and my younger brother. My younger brother never abused me. He tried to be a support as best as he could in that family, and in that house.

It had been years since I had seen my older brother, and no one knew where he was. I wasn't able to do anything with the estate until we tracked him down. I ended up having to take out an ad in the newspaper to find him. Eventually we did get in touch with him. All he wanted was his share of the money, and then he was out of the picture again. I didn't confront him at the time. I was still in a place where my feelings were bubbling under the surface. There certainly was rage there when I interacted with him, but we didn't talk about what had happened. Since then, no one has heard from him. I actually think he may have passed away.

After the money was distributed and my brother left, I was going through my mother's house and I found a letter she had written to him. I opened it. In the letter, she said how she loved him much more than my other brother and myself and that their secret would always be safe with her. And she gladly protected him through all of what went on with me. I was furious. She made me the executor of her estate because she didn't think anyone else in the family was reliable enough. And she left a letter like that where I could easily find it. It was like a knife in the back.

I've always believed that my mother had a sexual relationship with my brother. I also think that she had been sexually abused as a child herself, certainly by her father, if not by her uncles as well. None of this was ever talked about openly, though.

As a child, I hated my mom. I hated her. I moved out at twelve, because one of us was going to kill the other. That's how bad it was getting. Even then, I had this feeling that I didn't want to spend the rest of my life in jail over her. For someone like that. When I first moved out, she made me move back, but then I moved out for good when I was fourteen. I turned myself in to the juvenile justice system, so she could not take me back. I became a ward of the court. This infuriated her because in the game of chess, I had outsmarted her and it was checkmate. There was no longer anything she could do to control me.

I hated her so badly that from the time I was four or five years old, my whole goal was to get out of the house so that I could get away from her. I wanted away from her more than I wanted away from my brother who was molesting me.

She didn't sexually abuse me, but she did everything else. She abused me verbally, emotionally, and physically. She'd whack me with anything she had in her hand. When I was around twelve, I was at a neighbor's house and she grabbed me by the hair and physically dragged me on the ground all the way back to our house. Then she beat the shit out of me. I promised myself that would never ever, ever happen to me again.

After that, I started lifting weights at school and became stronger and stronger. Eventually, when I was fourteen, she tried to abuse me again but she didn't have a chance. We were fighting, I was the one on top. Suddenly, I realized that if this continued I was going to kill her.

During my healing process, I realized I had to forgive, not for them, but for me. I did a ritual on a full moon to help with releasing this hatred. I prepared a bath, sprinkled salt into it with the intention of having a clearing. I added some essential oils and things like that. I was so hurt and angry that I stayed in there for six hours. During those six hours, I really came to a point of understanding. I put myself in my mom's mind and body. What would I do in that situation? My son just raped my daughter. Would I turn in my son? What would I have done?

I realized that I couldn't answer that. I couldn't say what I would have done. I didn't know. That was such a tremendous choice point. It was like choosing a child to die.

I'm not saying what she did wasn't wrong. It was wrong. But this experience allowed me to understand the depth of the choice that she was dealing with. I also began to gain some understanding for my brother. To my recollection, it was the first time he ever drank alcohol and the first time he was drunk. After that, he was always drunk. And his friend was one of those friends you really wish your kids weren't friends with.

I came to a place of deep understanding. Did they make the right choices? No. Did they make the right choices for me? Absolutely not. But once I was able to understand on that level, forgiveness came easily. The forgiving and the release was easy.

I also see my healing as breaking a generational cycle of physical abuse. My husband and I actually almost got a divorce over this, because I said that we would never spank our kids. We would never harmfully touch our kids, period. This was a line in the sand, and I made it clear that if he crossed it, we were done.

The easy road is falling back into the cycle of abuse. The hard road is making a change. My boys are thirty-six and forty-one right now. They both thank me all the time for the way they were raised. They have friends who weren't raised with that same kindness. Forming a new pattern was hard, but during their childhoods I tried to talk things through with them in ways they could understand. Sometimes I would have to leave the room for a little bit if I was angry, because I knew I had to avoid the quick lash out response.

I want people to hear my story and understand that you can break that generational cycle. I also want people to know that you're not alone. I held this in and didn't tell anyone for fifty years because I thought I was alone, that I was the only person this had happened to. But you're not alone. You're not broken. And it's not your fault.

I think because I had cut myself off so fully from my feelings, I never ended up feeling like a victim. In some ways, this was good. Victim consciousness can be so hard to break. Not feeling like a victim helped me feel strong and autonomous, like I didn't need anybody. Now I'm working on balancing that, on letting people in.

In astrology, there's something called your north node, and it determines what your biggest challenge and your biggest lesson will be in this life. In my chart, my lesson is about actually feeling, truly *experiencing* your feelings. When I first learned this, I was like, "You've got to be kidding me. I will absolutely not go there." I was terrified of feeling my feelings, let alone talking about them. When I was raising my family, if a conflict came up it was basically, you go to your corner, you go to your corner, we don't talk about it, we're done. Everything is good, nobody gets hurt. Though I broke the major abuse cycles in my family, I do think there was some friction for my children being raised by parents who didn't do emotions. Maybe this disconnect from emotion is now my sons' cycle to break. Even in the best circumstances, we all end up with habits from our parents that we seek to grow from as adults. I know, though, that the things my sons have to heal are not the wounds of sexual abuse and violence that I had as a child. If there is any good that came out of those experiences, it is that I was able to do things differently for my sons.

To me, healing modalities are like spokes on a wheel. Whichever spoke you pick, whatever you resonate with the most is your path, and it's going to lead you to the center. The center is you. For me, astrology, numerology, and diving deeply into various spiritual traditions helped me to understand myself on a deep level, and to realize why certain things were happening in my life. I'm so analytical and my ego was so strong. The walls around my heart were so big and thick. My childhood left me with a very good idea of the things I didn't want. It has taken me a long time to figure out the things I *do* want.

I want to connect. I want to feel my feelings, I want to explore my emotions, I want to live truthfully and authentically. And because of this, I want to share my story.

PART 3

I SURVIVED

*"God never gives us more than we can handle.
I sure hope that is true.*

*Even through all the unspeakable pain and suffering, there
can be light at the end of the tunnel.*

I hope that you will find light and love."

—My prayer for you

CHAPTER 9

LIZ

"I want to tell women to keep fighting to get what they deserve. Protect your child, protect yourself and don't accept anything less."

Having gone through the most painful experience of my life, watching my daughter go through the horrible situation of molestation by her father, has led me to want to make a difference in the lives of other mothers who experience something similar. I know how prevalent molestation is, and it is my hope to provide love and support and healing for mothers and children who have unfortunately had this horrific act occur in their lives.

When I was about eleven, two older boys attempted to rape me. I fought tooth and nail, and was able to get away. I kicked and screamed and fought. I remember one of them yelling at the other to hold me down. It's an imprint on my memory that I'll never forget. There were other situations later on where I experienced date rape, or felt so pressured into sex that I participated in it even though I absolutley did not want to. But the experience that has been most traumatizing was what happened to my daughter. She was molested from infancy until the time that she was about three and a half.

Her biological father, who is no longer her father in all the ways that matter, was my boyfriend. By the time I gave birth to her, he and I were already broken up. I was always a single mother. During the last portion of our relationship I saw how angry he could be. I was scared of him. I was worried that perhaps in the future, when she was a teenager or something, he might end up losing his temper and hitting her. I never in my wildest dreams considered that he would hurt her as a baby. I never imagined this. I did get a sense that something was wrong before my daughter actually told me what was happening. I had a mother's intuition that something wasn't right, but I didn't understand it.

When Mike and I started dating, I knew he struggled with anger. I'm a transformational coach, and I'm very interested in the human psyche and people's ways of being. I could tell that he suffered from depression, and thought his anger was a symptom of that. I came to learn that when he became angry it was almost like a second personality. Being the healer that I am, I felt bad for him. I had a heart for his struggles, and I thought if he could work through them we would be okay. He also wasn't very sexually interested in me. This was hard for me, because I was attracted to him and I wanted to be very sexually active in our relationship. I didn't understand why he wasn't attracted to me. I'm a pretty conventionally attractive woman. I was around thirty-nine at the time, and was in great shape and at the height of my journey with taking care of myself. Looking back now, I understand that he wasn't attracted to me because his attraction was all about control. He couldn't control me. We ended up taking a trip to South America, and that's where I really saw his other side. He could be the sweetest, kindest, nicest person, but then his other side would come out and he would be incredibly mean. Being the strong woman that I am, I knew that once we got back to the States I would have nothing to do with him again. After we returned, I washed my hands of him. I thought, "I'll never have to see him again, thank God." And six weeks later, I found out I was pregnant.

From that time on, I was very worried that the road ahead would be challenging. I was scared of him during the pregnancy. He would go back and forth between being supportive and verbally abusive. Our eventual shared custody was never comfortable. I tried to soothe myself by saying he's a good guy. He would do fun things with her, and there was certainly a fun side to him that I'd enjoyed when we dated. I wanted her to be able to experience that. I didn't want to take her from her father, but I knew in my heart of hearts that something was wrong. I just didn't trust him, and I didn't know why. I talked myself out of this discomfort. "What's he going to do? She's a baby. His mother is helping him, his girlfriend is helping him. Everything is fine." I thought I was being overly protective, and I didn't want to be an overprotective mother. But she would come back and she was not herself. I thought that maybe she was just overtired, or didn't want to leave Mom. When she got a little older, she'd wake up in her car seat and scream "No, no, no." She could barely talk at this time. She would act so scared. I was also a first-time mother. I didn't know what was normal and what wasn't.

It became more confusing as she grew. She would go through periods of not wanting to see him, but then he'd show up and he'd be kind of fun and friendly and playful. And then she'd go through periods where she really looked forward to seeing him. I fully turned around in the car once because she said, "I want to stay with dad tonight." That had never happened before. I wanted to fully support her having a positive relationship with her father, so I would make sure they had time together. I would go out of my way to get her to see him, especially when he was also expressing real interest in her. I've come to learn that sometimes victims, though I hate to call anyone that, can actually continue to love the person who is hurting them. This is part of the reason it ends up being so emotionally confusing for them. Someone they love is abusing them, but they still want to be loved. Every little girl wants their father's love. She did crave a relationship with him, even though she was scared of the abuse.

Looking back, I've come to understand that there were signs. When she used to scream, it wasn't just like a child not wanting to go to school or something. It was this real scream of horror. Those days, it would break my heart to have to turn her over to him, but I had to due to legal placement. I knew she felt unsafe, and so I would give her a toy and tell her it was magical and that she could hug it when she needed to. I can't stress enough that I was a first-time mom, and I'd never really been around babies before I had my own. I didn't know what to expect.

I ended up breastfeeding fairly late. I think this was in part an intuitive response to comfort her due to my intuition around what was happening with her father, but also I'm a pretty naturalistic kind of mom. When she was about two and a half, she would scream and scream to nurse again after coming home from a weekend with him. In horror and panic, she screamed, "Milk! Milk!" and pawed at my chest like her life depended on it. After trying to soothe her and rock her without any change, I gave in. Magically, my milk came back immediately and we continued to nurse again after that. Now, I understand that she had probably just been through a horrific weekend with him and needed some comfort from her mother. I told myself that if this is what would help her, then it was the least I could do.

She was around three and a half when she came back from visiting him and said, "Mom, you need to check my bottom." I asked why, and she said, "Because Daddy put his finger in it." Even then, I still tried to rationalize it. He must have been wiping her. Or maybe she had a rash. In hindsight, there was a lot going on with her behavior that was due to what was happening to her. She needed a lot more care because of what she was going through. There were moments she was in anguish, squeezing her own arms and crying in the corner, wondering why she was such a bad girl. She made comments about not wanting to live. She wasn't even four years old at this time.

He will never be fully aware of the damage he did to her. I can only imagine he thought she wouldn't be affected by or know what he was doing, as she was just a baby, toddler and small girl. But the effects are tremendously painful and damaging. It was beyond heartbreaking to watch.

The first person I told was the director of the child care program she was in. I was so confused at what I should do. I had just repaired my relationship with her father after some previous conflict, and knew if I accused him of this all hell would break loose. His reaction would be nothing short of insanity and anger. She told me that in these kinds of situations, it was mandatory for her to report it, but if I were to promise that we would go see a doctor and book an appointment that day, she wouldn't report it yet. I had no idea what to do. I didn't understand how the doctor would even be able to determine whether she'd been touched or not. The program director said, "Just go. They have things that they can do." So I picked her up early and we made an appointment.

The doctor told us that everything was fine physically, but she was also required to report it. I could tell she wanted to stay out of it. She didn't really ask my daughter any questions. My daughter did tell a nurse that she was there because daddy had touched her bottom. The nurse never made a report of this, and eventually the doctor even said that she wouldn't report it if I had a conversation with him about it in person. I told her to give me a day or two to do this, because I hated having to see him in person. Because she wasn't an expert in this area, she also suggested that we go to a specialist.

I started the conversation with him by complimenting him on being a great father, and the things that he did well while parenting our daughter. I was so scared. I was scared of him, and I was scared of what would happen if it were true. If he'd been touching her. I told him what she'd said, and he laughed very hard. I remember it as almost an evil laugh. He said, "I don't go near that area." This was obviously a lie. I'm a single mom, he's a single dad. Yes, he had a girlfriend but she wasn't always there, and you do have to go near that area of a child to bathe them and change diapers. I asked him if maybe she'd had a rash or something, and he said "Nope, nothing. I don't know. I don't go near it." Even then, I was in denial. I was relieved, I could tell the doctor that he didn't do it.

Looking back, I have to ask why every person here seemed to be trying to protect him, even me. None of us want to believe someone we know is capable of raping a child, and yet with the numbers of people who are molested or raped, it is clear that someone is doing the raping. It is hard to believe that anyone could be capable of something like this, but a disturbing number of people are capable, and commit these acts of violence repeatedly.

That same night, I picked my daughter up from daycare. On the way home, I told her that we'd be going on vacation to Florida soon. I mentioned that we could go see her grandmother, her dad's mom. She had a place down there. I said that maybe we would invite Daddy. She started freaking out, screaming no over and over again. I could not get her to calm down. Finally, I pulled into my driveway and rushed around to the back seat to get her out of her car seat. She stared me in the face and said, "Daddy put his finger in my vagina, and it hurt." I stopped in my tracks.

I said, "Honey, I understand. If that is true, it's a very good thing that you told me that. But if it is not true, you can't say it."

She looked at me and said, "Mom, it's true." This is a three-and-a-half-year-old girl. At that moment, I was covered in goosebumps. I couldn't deny what was happening anymore. There's no way she would have this large of a reaction, and no way she would make this up or even have the language to make it up. I knew I had to call the doctor and tell her everything.

The doctor told us that we would have to do a forensic interview. I called the child advocacy center, and they told me that it would take a week or two before we were able to do the interview. I wanted to do it as quickly as possible. When we did get an appointment for the interview, we had to drive two hours to get to the child advocacy center. During the interview, she clearly stated the facts around what had happened to her. She even laid on the floor with her knees apart and demonstrated what he did to her. She had these kind of crazy eyes while she did it. It was a very, very odd, painful experience as a mother. I made the choice not to listen to the interview when it was conducted. I couldn't bear to know any more. I ended up seeing it years later when it was shown in court, and at the time they told me that she did a good job, and that the evidence was clear. Unable to watch the recording, I asked the interviewer to explain what she had told them. She had described a pink, battery-operated device being used on her body.

I had such a visceral reaction. I screamed, and cried, and yelled, "I knew it. Fuck him! I knew it was true."

Before the interviewer confirmed my worst fears, I still continually questioned myself. I still couldn't believe it really happened to her or that this was really happening to us. But at that moment, the part of me that still wanted to deny what was happening fell away. Because of this experience, I can imagine how some mothers make the horrible choice to ignore the truth when their own baby is being harmed. It's not that any mother would want this to happen, or allow this to happen. It is that there isn't a single mother that wants to *believe* that this could be happening to their beloved child.

I'm very spiritual, and I believe that there are signs for us that can guide and lead us. Shortly before the forensic interview, I was on a Zoom call talking to my therapist about everything that was happening with my daughter. As I was discussing the details with my therapist, through the window I saw this huge cat. It was a lynx. It was gray and about two feet tall. It was nothing like a housecat cat, it was much larger, so clearly wild, and its ears had these big fluffy tops. It was just sitting there, staring at me. Very few people will ever see a lynx, they're quite reclusive. Later I looked up the spiritual meaning of the lynx, and they're thought to be seers of truths, and that if you see one it means that secrets are being revealed. I saw the lynx again one other time, while I was talking to a coach of mine about this topic. I've only ever seen one when discussing what happened to my daughter, which may sound a little woo-woo to you but, to me it was a beautiful sign because at the time I was so scared. I was scared to be in my home. I was sure that her father was going to find out about the forensic interview and do something. I don't know what I thought would happen exactly, but if he knew he might be going to prison for child molestation he might kill himself and perhaps kill me first. He's been suicidal in the past. I couldn't sleep in that house, so I went to stay at a friend's. I was a wreck. I couldn't handle the emotions I was experiencing. It's like I was in a constant state of panic, fear and anxiety. I was in fight or flight every moment. Not just for those first weeks and months, but for the next several years so we went to live in California for some time and it took me years to come back to my home. Even after that, I would still get uncomfortable thinking that in any store or public place, I might run into him. I didn't even want to go out to dinner. Honestly, I still don't. Everyone in this town seems to know our story, and it is incredibly painful. I lost friends. Some people took his side and said I made this up to get custody of my daughter. How horrible of a person would I be to do such a thing? How could anyone think that of me?

It was painful enough to go through what we were experiencing as my daughter continually struggled due to the abuse, but that pain was compounded by knowing that there were judgments all around us. That people who could have been supporting me were doing the opposite. They will never know the pain they caused. And I know it is up to me to release myself from this pain, because no one else can.

The legal battle for custody of my daughter took almost three years. I finally won. The criminal case is another story entirely. I thought that because of what he'd done, he'd end up going to prison for child molestation. They did charge him with incest, and the women who did the forensics interview suggested to me that he might get up to forty years. But he didn't end up spending even a single night in jail. He was arrested, which is why what happened to my daughter ended up in the news and why that has been a continuing source of trauma for us. He did have a large bond set, I think it was around ten thousand dollars. His girlfriend bailed him out. The DA ended up not wanting to press charges. Because the DA prosecutes these cases, I didn't get to have an attorney other than the DA or get to have counsel outside of her and her team. She was young and timid and kept telling us that these cases are really hard to prove. She didn't want to use any of the evidence. Because the doctor was a mandatory reporter and didn't report, what happened at the doctor's office apparently didn't have evidentiary value. I also felt as though the DA didn't really believe me. She would ask me the same questions over and over again, suggesting that perhaps I'd brought my daughter to the doctor due to a rash. I blame myself more than the pediatrician. I didn't know what questions to ask and didn't want to rock the boat. Still, things might have been different if a report had been made. He eventually ended up with a lesser charge, and just a year's probation. I let the DA and the court reporter know that allowing this lesser charge set a precedent for every woman out there that's been abused, that there's nothing the court will do about it, and that we're still weak in the eyes of the law. I was enraged that the court lets this happen to women and children. I was enraged by the whole process. If nothing happened to him, he was going to keep doing this to her. I've now learned that molesters groom children, and that's exactly what he'd been doing. Eventually, this leads to intercourse as the child gets older if it isn't stopped. I'm going to say this harshly, because the truth here is horrible but important. My daughter would have ended up getting fucked by her father. And the court threw their hands in the air and said, "Well, there's really nothing we can do." If the civil court hadn't sided with me, he would have ended up getting fifty-fifty placement.

I wish I had more advice for parents dealing with these types of issues. Don't try to discourage the doctor from filing the mandatory report as they are obligated to do. In fact, I strongly encourage asking the doctor directly if they will be taking care of the mandatory reporting. Even if you're uncertain whether a crime occurred (naturally none of us wants to believe it could be true), and even if the doctor doesn't find physical evidence such as a broken hymen (molestation does not necessarily leave physical evidence), *you still* need the doctor to document and report your suspicions. Perhaps if I had recorded what happened at the doctor's office, assuming they even would have allowed me to record, things would have been different. But it doesn't seem like there was a lot I could have done to better navigate that system. The good news is that even when criminal court doesn't work out, family court can. We had to fight so hard, and provide our own evidence, and document everything. We had to keep presenting that evidence over and over again, and keep our story consistent, even though we were telling the truth. When these things happen, it is so easy to get confused because you're in emotional trauma. Even though you're telling the truth, you need to write things down and rehearse your story—not because it is a story, but because attorneys will use any tiny inconsistencies to insist that you're lying. I went through two male attorneys that kept insisting there was very little we could do, that my daughter would have some degree of placement with her father no matter what. I heard this again and again. I thought, "Over my dead body." Honestly, if I had to leave the country and go AWOL, I was going to do it. My parents, her grandparents, would miss us terribly but if I had to disappear to protect her, I would have. I could not let this keep happening to my daughter.

I struggled with questioning myself. So many people questioned me that it was hard to keep those voices out and stay secure in the truth. There was pain in knowing his arrest and what he had done got out on the news, and knowing that there are people in my community that didn't believe my daughter and didn't believe me. Truly, there were people who said that I was a crazy bitch who made all of this up to get custody, that I was a piece of shit for being the type of woman who would make all of this up. All I needed at the time was support. All I needed was people to say, "I'm so sorry this happened to you, how can we help you get through it?" But it felt as though the community turned against me. I had friends turn on me, and people who thought my three-and-a-half-year-old child was lying.

When I finally got a female attorney who had been a victim herself, I knew I was with the right person. She was willing to fight for us and tell our story. I could tell she loved my daughter, and the financial help from my loved ones made working with her possible. If I could give any advice around this, I would say that there are resources out there that you're not yet aware of. Ask for help, and don't give up. I would also recommend going to a therapist immediately after there's been evidence of abuse, and go regularly. The therapist we went to was able to share evidence she had found in our sessions, which really helped the case. The forensic interviewer also shared evidence. With all this evidence, including the police investigations, the guardian ad litem was really listening to us. Eventually, I also took the stand. My daughter didn't have to, due to her age and the fact that we had a forensic interview done. I was able to get full custody.

Going through several attorneys in order to get effective counsel in family court was very costly. Right before we were about to go to court, I got another bill from the attorney and I couldn't pay it. I was already in debt. I was desperate to be able to continue to work with the one attorney who had listened to us, who was willing to fight for us and tell our story. I sat out on my deck that night after my daughter went to bed. I looked up at the stars, and I prayed. I asked Spirit, "What am I going to do? I have to do something. I have to protect her. Oh, God, please help us."

In my mind, I heard the words, "Ask for help."

So I wrote a letter from my heart, and I sent it to three people: my mom and two friends.

One of these friends called me the next morning and said, "There'll be a $10,000 check in your mailbox today." It still gives me tears to think about it. My mom did the same thing.

It's been a very long road. His parental rights haven't been terminated fully yet, because it is very hard to get this done because I don't have a husband, which is bullshit. If I were married, I could go to the state and show them that someone wanted to adopt her, and at that point they might terminate his rights, but not before, because they really prioritize a child having two parents. I care for my daughter fully, I own my own business and make sure everything she needs is provided for. It is insane that this isn't enough to get sole parental rights. Before this, I was never that worried about my own death. Now, I'm very afraid that if something were to happen to me, he might still have a legal claim to her. In theory, he could still continue to challenge my custody, but since the ruling we haven't heard a word from him. This shows me again that he is guilty.

Even his behavior in court showed me his guilt. His mother and his girlfriend were at the hearing, and when the forensic interview was being discussed he insisted that it was private. The judge explained to him that it was sealed evidence, which meant that it was private outside the court but could be discussed within the court. But he didn't want anyone to see what was in the forensic interview, so the judge dismissed the galley from the court. His mother and girlfriend left, and never ended up seeing the evidence. They still want to believe he didn't do it, and that I'm this horrible person separating my daughter from her father. I understand that it is hard to believe that your son or loved one is capable of something like this. Before this happened, I didn't believe he was capable of something like this either, or I would never have left my daughter with him. Thankfully, my daughter hasn't ever had to see him since his arrest.

Part of my healing has been holding forgiveness for him. I have forgiven him, because I know that he must be in such a confused, sick, painful state to do something like this to a child. He's never had the tools to deal with the trauma that has occurred in his own life. He's never had that kind of support. He's never received the healing work. I strongly suspect he experienced sexual abuse as a child. My intuition tells me that it happened to him and his brother, and his mother buried her head in the sand. I'll never know for sure, but he certainly fits that profile.

My daughter has a lot of continuing struggles due to this abuse. I'm certain because of the evidence that came up that he used a vibrator on her. I also suspect that she climaxed. At age two or three, she used to try to show her vagina to my mother when we would video chat with her. She would fight to put her fingers in my vagina. She would get very distressed, and scream, "Why won't you let me do it? Mom, please, please. Just let me put my fingers in there." I would hold my legs together fighting my daughter's hands. She was trying to force her hands in between my thighs. Clearly not fucking normal behavior from a three-year-old. That same day she and I went skiing, and a woman from our town came up to me and accused me of lying about what had happened to my daughter. I was going through the deepest pain ever. I'd just been fighting to keep my daughter's fingers out of my vagina. And this lady was screaming at me. I mean, she truly raised her voice and screamed. I was already so shook up, it was like she kicked me when I was down. All I really needed was a hug. What I really needed was someone to say, "You're going to be okay," because I didn't know if we would be okay. After that, I became so scared to be in public.

I don't like to have her in the school and this community. We will probably end up moving again. But being in this community means I'm closer to family. It's a big decision to pick up and completely change your life, and we've already gone through so much. Thankfully, her father lives about an hour away and I haven't seen him outside of court. I can go to my workout classes and get groceries without being too frightened of running into him. I used to go see live music and occasionally go to dinner in the town close to where he lives, but now I won't. I won't be going back there for a very long time. It really impacts your life regardless of the community response, but the publicness of what happened to us is also incredibly difficult.

Even though we've gone through so much, I want other women to know that if you stay strong, if you stay committed to healing and protection, if you allow yourself kindness, then there is a light at the end of the tunnel. I can say that my daughter and I now are completely protected, and we are happy. I have a thriving business that supports us both and is only thriving because I've been able to take care of myself emotionally through this. It was very hard to keep it together during the process. We still have our challenges. Reading and writing have been hard for her, and she's very behind in school. She struggles with attention issues. I'll never know if it's because of this trauma, or just something that she struggles with. I believe there are so many effects that we'll never totally understand.

We're currently taking a break from therapy, because it became really hard on us. When we would go, she would fight and scream. It was too traumatic to keep reliving what happened to her. The therapist and I both decided it was time to take a break. I think at this young age, she doesn't need to be reliving the horrible incident and dealing with this right now. I think at some time, maybe in her adolescence or teens, she will absolutely get more support around this. But right now she is seven and a half. I think she gets a break.

I want women to know that you're not alone. I want to tell women to keep fighting to get what they deserve. Protect your child, protect yourself and don't accept anything less. Don't accept it when they tell you, "No, you're going to lose this case anyway, it's just your word against his." It's such patriarchal bullshit that the court system allows it to continue happening to women and children. I want to tell women to trust their intuition. You're not a mean or bad person to defend your child. Sadly, most of the time, the person who did this to your child is someone you trusted, someone you loved. It might have been your father, your uncle, your friend, your husband, the father of your child.

If you're going through this, lean on a trusted friend or two. Don't be afraid to ask for support from the kind, gentle-hearted people who love you. Also, seek professional therapy for your child and for yourself. Taking care of yourself through this is absolutely essential. Don't forget the simple things like meditation, journaling, going for a massage, giving yourself a spa day or just taking a warm bath. You're not just treating yourself, you're actually managing your central nervous system. Sometimes, the central nervous system needs outside help to find calm. If a glass of wine helps you calm down, have a glass of wine, but be cautious around numbing habits. If you find that you're getting too hooked on that glass of wine, it will create more anxiety and pain. You're not going to feel like you're being the mother you could be. During times of great trauma some of our worst habits can seem comforting, so take care of yourself, and stay mindful. Try to keep yourself and your energy healthy, but also give yourself grace. I'm a yoga teacher. I eat really healthy. I do cleanses. But when I was going through this, sometimes I would have a glass of wine and a cigarette and it was exactly what I needed. Prioritize what puts you in a state of calm and ease, because you're going to need your strength.

Give extra love to yourself and to your child. I have so much love for my little girl. I take every opportunity I can to react with gentleness, and to show her love. Try to be understanding, supportive, and so, so loving. Your child deserves that extra love, and so do you.

I wish the same for other women to trust yourself and protect your child above all else. Nothing else will ever matter as much as that. Never underestimate the damage this can do if it continues.

You have to do everything you can to be sure it never happens again.

If you need support, there are groups on Facebook that you can join to connect with others who are going through similar situations.

CHAPTER 10

MEL

"Even from a very young age I had this feeling that, as fucked up as my situation was, telling my story was going to benefit somebody else someday. That if I could just heal from it, my experience would help others. That's basically what kept me alive."

I'm forty-four, but I look younger. Some people think I'm in my thirties, which I always love. I was eight years old when I was first sexually abused. My mother left me alone in an RV with two older boys. One of them wanted me to give him a blow job, and tried to pressure me into it. I didn't end up doing it. I attempted to, though. It was traumatizing and disgusting. And I haven't attempted one since, I mean, I've never given a blow job. After that experience with these boys, I've had absolutely no interest. I'm not even sure how we knew these two boys, or whose family they were from. Maybe we were moving from one place to another. I have no fucking idea. My mother didn't make the most skillful choices with me. She left me in some really fucked up situations. This is really the core of my trauma. Other terrible things happened. I mean awful things, my brother abusing me, his death. I used to think that this was really what I was struggling with, But, I've done a lot of healing work and realized that it started with my mom.

The next instance I experienced was a guy from our neighborhood. He was this older guy who always hung out with kids. We always wound up hanging out with him and playing spin the bottle. He was a really creepy guy. I remember he would come up and knock on my door and ask to see my underwear. This happened on a somewhat regular basis. Once, we were under some sort of parking structure or something. He sort of asked like, "If I show you mine, will you show me yours?" I think he touched me, but nothing more than that happened. I think more traumatizing than the actual experience was what happened when I told my mom about it. When I told her, I was pretty hysterical. And in order to calm my hysteria, my mother smacked me across the face. Then we went to the police station to file a report. I don't remember much more of that. I don't know exactly how old he was, but way older than me. Maybe eighteen or twenty. And my mother would just let me hang out with him.

The experiences that had the most lasting impact on me were with my brother. This also began around when I was eight. He was about thirteen when he moved in with us. My brother and I have the same father, but different mothers. He was in foster care, and my father didn't help to get him out, but my mother did. She really tried to help him. He had an extreme temper. He would throw things. He once flipped over and smashed a whole glass coffee table. I was definitely scared of him. My mother worked third shift, and so she left me overnight with him. He started playing a sort of wrestling game with me, but it involved touching private parts. If he was able to, he would give me inappropriate back rubs and he would finger me. Eventually, it escalated to the point where he would perform oral sex on me. This didn't happen too frequently, as he was in and out of foster care. But it did happen at least two or three times.

Years later, once he was an adult, I actually went to live with him. He really wanted me to come live with him, and I couldn't stand living with my mother anymore. He was so proud. He made sure I went to school, and did my homework, all of that. But then he started to have remorse about what he had done to me. He started to feel guilty. Eventually, he asked me, "Did what I do to you affect you?" I was still terrified of him at the time, and so I told him no.

But God works in mysterious ways. Soon after that, I was over at a friend's house. Her mom was teaching me study skills because I had a hard time focusing in school. My friend and her mother knew I was living with my brother. They started asking me questions about if I was okay, where I was sleeping, that sort of stuff. It got super, super uncomfortable for me. When they eventually dropped me off at my brother's house, they gave me a quarter so that if I needed to call them from a payphone I could. My brother wasn't home when I got there, so I walked into town to where he usually hung out with his friends. When my brother saw me, there was this look on my face. He asked me what was wrong, and I told him, "Well, what you did actually did affect me." I think maybe I had already called my friend and her mother to pick me up when I was walking into town, or maybe I called them shortly after. They came to get me, and he said that he would pack my stuff for me and I could come by tomorrow and get it.

The next day, my friend's dad went with me to get my stuff. There was a note on the door that said, "Door's open, come in." And when I opened the door, he was hanging in his living room.

He left a suicide note that said, "I sinned, I'm sorry. And I leave all my belongings to my sister." I wound up inheriting everything he owned. I don't remember feeling anything when I opened the door and found him. I was numb. I didn't even cry. I was in shock. And then I had this thought. As I looked at him hanging there, it was the first time I had ever seen him look peaceful. After we found him, we drove to the police station, and I got to call my dad and give him the news that his son had committed suicide. I haven't liked talking on the phone ever since.

I went to live with that friend and her parents after that. I began to shed my entire identity. My mother named me Melinda and called me Mindy. In my mind, Mindy died when my brother died. I began to take on my brother's identity. It was like he took over my body. I started walking and talking like him. Because I inherited all of his stuff, I started wearing his clothes. I planned to commit suicide just like he did. I didn't give a fuck. I was already in a really dark place before his suicide. The year before, I'd been put in juvenile detention for running away from home. I already wasn't doing great. My brother's death was almost the nail in my coffin. I don't really remember it all that well, but I ended up jumping off a balcony. Because of this, my high school kicked me out and said I couldn't come back until I got intensive therapy. I got sent to a psychiatric ward for evaluation. And I spent a month there and they were like, "No, you're not ready to go home." Then, they sent me to a diagnostics center for another thirty days and the diagnostics center was like, "No, you're still not ready to go home." So they shipped me off to a residential treatment center for emotionally disturbed youth. And I spent the next year and a half of my life living there. I was fifteen when my brother died, and I was eighteen when I graduated from the treatment center.

After I left the treatment center, I started smoking crack. It's not that unusual that I struggled after leaving the treatment program. I became institutionalized. When you become institutionalized and you get out, you go right back to where you were before you went in. So I just went right back to using drugs, and doing all the crap I had done with my brother in the past. During this time, I always hung out with older adults. There were some really important people in my life who took me under their wing. There was one woman who ended up putting the fear of god in me. She noticed what I was doing—it was pretty clear. She wanted to beat the shit out of me for what I was doing to myself. So I stopped doing crack. I was still doing LSD, and smoking weed, and honestly anything else I could get my hands on, you know, ecstasy and shit like that.

At nineteen, I got married. I met him when I was sober and then we relapsed together. He was a crack addict. Every once in a while, he just wouldn't come home for a couple of days, and he'd blow his whole paycheck and go on a crack binge. That relationship lasted all of three years. He actually tried to commit suicide the same was my brother did. We were separated, I was living at my dad's house and I knew something wasn't right. I went to my husband's house, and there he was, hanging from the light fixture with his Nike jacket in the fucking dining room or in the living room or whatever. The door was locked, but I got in through the window. For perspective, my husband was ten years older than me and jacked. Like, huge. He got out of prison after spending six years for involuntary manslaughter. And I am a twig, maybe 115 pounds. I tried to get him down, and he fell from the light fixture. He was on crack, and I managed to keep him down as he threw up. I didn't want him to get up and hurt himself. I managed to hold him down and called 911 and kept him on the ground until the cops and paramedics arrived. When they walked in the door and saw me holding him down they were fucking blown out of the water that I was able to hold him down. This incident is what truly ended our marriage.

After that, I realized I liked girls. I hate labels. They imply permanence. Since I started dating women, I've never been attracted to a man. Generally, I'm attracted to the human body. If I see a really good looking guy, I appreciate his looks, but it doesn't make me want to be with him. I don't like to label myself lesbian, bisexual, whatever. I just fall in love with whoever I fall in love with. And it's only ever been women since 1999.

My healing process took years and years and years. It really started at the residential treatment center, because that's where I was introduced to yoga and mindfulness and started to become willing to look within at all the trauma. All the pain, all the suffering, like all of it. Before that, I didn't have any way to really process it. My parents didn't bring me up in church, but my mom's best friend started taking me to a Baptist church with her when I was around eight. Because I'm a seeker, I soaked it all in like a sponge and accepted Jesus into my heart. I even tried to help convert people. After my brother's suicide, someone from the church told me he was burning in hell. That took me away from the church. I was like, fuck, this doesn't answer any of my questions anymore. I do still appreciate Christianity. I see it as a stepping stone for me. I've realized that I can have a personal relationship with God, and I don't really need an intermediary.

Eventually, I got interested in Buddhism, and learned about the bodhisattva vow. In it, you vow to keep incarnating, lifetime after lifetime, until all sentient beings are relieved of suffering and free from the cycle of karma, birth, death and rebirth. Even if you could achieve enlightenment and break out of this cycle yourself, you vow to wait, to keep coming back, until all living beings are able to achieve enlightenment. I feel as though I've taken that vow.

It took me a long time to step into my power and to stop playing small. For a long time, I thought I had caused my brother to kill himself. I thought I had caused my parents to separate. I thought my power, who I was, caused my mother to abandon me over and over again. I've finally learned to stop playing small, to stop stepping away from my power, and to fully embody it. Because of this, even from a very young age I had this feeling that, as fucked up as my situation was, telling my story was going to benefit somebody else someday. That if I could just heal from it, my experience would help others. That's basically what kept me alive. It's taken a lot of therapy. It's taken learning to connect to my physical body through yoga and mindfulness. It's taken a lot of therapy. It's taken learning to connect to my physical body through yoga and mindfulness. Early in my sobriety, I did a twelve-step program, which helped. But I think I've been able to sustain my healing because of my connection to my spirituality. It hasn't been easy. I struggled with drugs, but also with cutting. When I was younger, I was diagnosed with bipolar disorder, but later was diagnosed with borderline personality disorder. Getting this new diagnosis was freeing at the time. One of the signs is having really, really intense emotions, and I've always experienced that. Knowing my diagnosis helped me know what to expect and to manage what I was experiencing at the time. But there's also a core philosophy in Buddhism that nothing is permanent. I've given up so many labels. Now I know that, yes, perhaps I'm exhibiting symptoms, but I'm not necessarily going to be that way forever. It's not who I am. It's not permanent, nothing is. Knowing these experiences aren't permanent has helped me overcome them.

My ex-wife is the person who helped me shift some of the last pieces of my attachment issues, and also to stop self-harming. It was an unhealthy marriage in many ways, but she did help with those behaviors profoundly. It was for the best that the marriage didn't last. I was too much for her. My light was too bright. She always felt like I was stealing her stage. For the first six years of our marriage, I shut down in an attempt to be the person she wanted me to be. I stopped reading anything spiritual, I stopped meditating, I stopped connecting to my body in any way, and just played small. All I did was go to work and take care of her. She was always depressed and anxious. Eventually, I got to a point where I was like, I don't want to be here anymore. And I'm either going to end my life right now and be done with it and just come back in another body and start all over again, or I'm going to do whatever it takes to experience my birthright, which I know is to be happy and abundant in every area of my life.

That was the first moment that I started choosing me again. It took another six years to unmatch myself from the relationship but the more and more I started putting myself first, the farther and farther apart we got. I ended up having to lie to her to do a Marketing Mastery program. I was really committed to my own improvement, and she didn't feel the same. She didn't believe that I should start my own business. When we met, she'd been sober, but she started drinking again. Things got worse and worse. We were triggering each other all the time. Eventually, I was like, "I'm going to call it. I'm moving out." We haven't spoken since. My life has gotten a lot better since I left. So many things I thought of as symptoms I was experiencing due to my own trauma, ended up being symptoms of a bad relationship. Now I think that perhaps that relationship was on its own a symptom from some of the trauma I've experienced. It's one I'm glad to be free of.

Since then, I've been able to truly commit to myself. I started going to the gym and I tried rock climbing. I completely fell in love with it. I tried going vegan for a year, but it was too rigid. Now, intermittent fasting supports my work around keeping my body healthy and strong. I'm in the best shape of my life. I fully committed to my business, and even though COVID hit in 2020 it was the best year my business had ever had up to that point. I started investing in coaches and other people who could support me. One of them told me I should write a book, so I did. I wrote my book in seven weeks, and it has helped my business skyrocket.

When I think of my brother, my heart breaks for him. He had such a traumatic upbringing himself that all he knew was to abuse people. He didn't know anything different. His mother was extremely abusive. If my dad came home late, she would throw my infant brother against the wall. Who does that? She would hold a knife to my dad's throat. So that's what his early life looked like. He was severely abused, and then he was abandoned. He also experienced abuse in foster care. He was always abused and always traumatized. My heart breaks for him. He didn't have a fucking chance in hell. And so, I don't blame him for what he did. He didn't know any better. And he did have remorse. He was just so fucking confused. He used to tell me growing up that if I wasn't his sister, I'd be his girlfriend. As fucked up as that is, it also shows how much we were connected. I have total forgiveness for him. In an energetic healing session I had, he actually came through and let me know that it's okay to be happy. It's okay to move on, to live my best life, to become the best version of myself. He wants me to be happy. And so do I. I want me to be happy. Happiness and abundance and success is my birthright, and nothing and no one can ever take that away.

If you or anyone that you know is suicidal, please call 988 for help.

CHAPTER 11

MADISON

"I can't tell you how many times I walked around the
block and just prayed and prayed and prayed
and prayed and prayed."

I am fifty-five. When I was thirty-eight my husband and I fostered two children. We wanted to have a family so badly but we were unable to get pregnant so when we got the opportunity to foster, we felt so blessed. We first fostered Emily when she was two and Chase when he was three. After some time, we were eventually able to adopt them.

When presented with the opportunity to foster, the agency wanted us to take all the siblings. There were five in the family but we had our hands full with two. The reason we chose Emily and Chase was because they were the only two who shared the same mother and father.

I knew going in that there had been sexual abuse in their birth family, but because they were only two and three when we took them in, I didn't know how much this would end up affecting them. I did know their little eight-year-old sister had been raped, so perhaps I should have guessed that the sexual trauma in the family was severe and that it would impact them greatly, but this was over twenty-five years ago. The agencies had started to offer services but no one was really talking about stuff like this. It just wasn't a conversation people were having.

There is a law in California that if you have a baby while on drugs and it is is born with drugs in its system, the baby is automatically taken from you. That is why Emily and Chase were in foster care. When the birth mom was pregnant with her fifth baby, she got clean and took Emily and Chase back, which broke our hearts. A year later she went back to using, and all of her kids were taken away and her rights were terminated. We were finally able to get Emily and Chase back so that we could start our family. Six months later we officially adopted them. We were so happy! Emily had just turned four and Chase was five.

While the kids were back with their birth mom, we had no idea what was happening to them or how they were being treated. We had no contact so when the kids were returned, we were not aware of any sexual abuse. Sadly, during grade school, junior high and high school, they started acting out and it became clear that there had been abuse during the time they were returned to their birth mother.

When Emily was around nine and Chase was around ten, we moved to a new city. We found an amazing neighborhood and lived on this wonderful cul-de-sac, the kind where all the families know one another, barbecue together and watch each other's kids. The kids were able to run around, ride their bikes and just be kids. The moms hung out together, played bunco and enjoyed laughing and drinking wine on warm summer evenings.

Emily was desperate to make new friends, as any kid would be after moving to a new place, and she became friends with a girl named Kelsey. I didn't know it at the time, but Kelsey—who was only about a year older than Emily and just a little child herself—started acting out, and she molested Emily from when she was nine until she was about eleven. Kelsey called it their "secret game." Even though she was only a year older than Emily, Kelsey seemed more mature and sadly knew too much of the world. Her parents were often absent, and she spent a lot of time with her grandparents who lived just up the street from us. Due to Emily's history of neglect, she was very immature for her age and was easily manipulated. Around this cul-de-sac, there were about eight little girls, and most of them were younger than Emily and Kelsey. As little girls do, they all wanted to be included in everything. They would play dolls together, ride bikes and just do fun girly things. One of the little girls, who was about five years old, got wind of the secret game and wanted to know what it was. I truly think that my daughter wasn't at a developmental stage where she understood what she was doing was wrong, but Emily started playing the secret game with her. In the game, they touched each other and did a lot of inappropriate things. I had no idea any of this was going on.

Fast-forward about a year, and as I mentioned, all the moms hung out and we were all very good friends but I became especially close with the mother of this five-year-old girl. She had recently had another baby, so her daughter would come to our house to play all the time.

That summer, I took all the neighborhood kids, including the five-year-old, to vacation bible school camp. During camp, one of the lessons was to always tell the truth and that secrets were bad. So, the secret game comes out. The five-year-old came home and told her mom about the secret game. Her mother came over and told me what had happened. It was awful. I mean, what do you do in a situation like that? I immediately called CPS. I knew that this was very bad. How do you react? So many thoughts go through your head. How could this have happened? There is no way my child could have done something like this. How would she even know? How do I even talk to her about this? I took Emily for a hike alone and confronted her about it. At first, she denied knowing about the secret game, but eventually she admitted what had happened. She told me about Kelsey and the secret game. I asked her if she had played the game with any of the other neighborhood kids but she told me that it only happened with Kelsey and the one little girl.

Once Emily told me what was happening, her relationship with Kelsey began to make more sense. They had a very tumultuous relationship. Either they were best friends, or somebody was going to tell the other person's secret. They were always fighting.

After I called CPS, they got in touch with the police. Both my daughter and the five-year-old talked to the detectives. When I spoke to them, I tried to explain that I felt as though they were all just little kids, and that of course it was a mistake, but these were children. It didn't have to be seen as criminal. They told me that they still had to write a report and send it to the department because it was an older child with a younger child. But the detectives were so nice to Emily. She told them things she hadn't even told me. The detectives said that they didn't think anything would come of it, because they were both kids.

When the little girl's parents found out about everything, they were both distraught. They both took leaves of absence from their jobs. We had to tell the little girl to stop coming over to our house. They didn't even want Emily to play outside in our yard because they thought even seeing Emily from a distance would further traumatize their daughter. Their reaction is understandable, but I do think some of the intensity around the response made it worse for their daughter and made the whole experience more traumatizing. I offered to pay for their daughter's therapy. I felt so terrible about it.

I ended up going to all of our neighbors to tell them about what had happened. I went to everyone in my family and everyone we were friends with who had young kids and who Emily hung out with. It was incredibly difficult to have these conversations, to tell them what Emily had done and ask them to have a talk with their children and ask them if anything had happened to them. Eventually, we moved out of the neighborhood. Partly because we knew we couldn't keep Emily inside for the rest of her life, but mostly because the five-year-old was having nightmares and the neighbors had asked us to move. All of this was awful for our family. I loved the neighborhood and all of the neighbors, it was really hard on all of us.

Kelsey never experienced any consequences for participating in the game that I know of. Not that I think she should have, but considering how many consequences Emily faced for her actions it struck me as really unfair. The district attorney decided to press charges against Emily, due to the difference in age between her and the five-year-old. I was shocked. I mean, I was the one who called CPS. I thought the parents of the five-year-old and I were on the same page. I fully understood the severity of Emily's actions, but I didn't think it would end up in court. She was still a young child herself. The DA believed that Emily was going to continue offending. They made her out to be an evil child. Luckily, because she was underage, none of this is on Emily's record. She was on probation, though. She went through a year and a half of therapy for sexually inappropriate behavior. Emily ended up being on probation until she was a sophomore or junior in high school. They kept extending her probation if she got bad grades, or acted up in school. The extensions weren't because she had acted out sexually, they were for unrelated things. We had to go to court all the time and therapy session after therapy session. In addition to probation, therapy and all the court dates, Emily could never babysit or be left alone with children. I had to write reports to all of her schools that explained that she could never be paired with a younger child during a group project. In many ways, it took over our lives. I think this is why it was so hard to see the difference between how Emily and Kelsey were treated. Kelsey's dad was a police officer, so part of me wonders whether that was a factor. The one conversation I had with Kelsey's mother was really odd. When I called her and told her about it, she acted like it was no big deal at all. As if I was the third, fourth or fifth person to bring it to her attention. It was as if this was something she already knew. I had to tell her CPS would be calling, and she was still unfazed. It was such a weird reaction.

Unfortunately, about three years ago my niece, Hannah, came forward and told us that Emily had molested her. This molestation took place when Emily was around ten to twelve, around the same time she was playing the secret game with the five-year-old from our neighborhood. Hannah is a year younger than Emily. This has had a profound effect on our family. I have apologized a million times but there is still so much animosity. Emily says she doesn't remember touching her cousin. I don't know whether she actually does remember and is saying she doesn't, or if she truly can't recall doing it. Hannah went through a lot of counseling, and during one of her sessions she wrote a letter to me and Emily, telling us what had happened and expressing how she felt about it. And I wrote a letter back, apologizing profusely, but also explaining that this had also happened to Emily. I wrote that I was so sorry about what Emily did, but Emily was a victim, too. I also explained that Emily says she doesn't remember, and that she was welcome to write her a letter but I didn't know what response she would get. I do understand that a good apology doesn't come with a "but." I was hoping that hearing that Emily experienced something similar would help Hannah be able to understand that even though what happened was horrible, Emily was hurting, too. Emily was still very young, and very immature. She didn't understand how wrong it was to be doing what she was doing.

The family was very upset that I stuck up for Emily. They saw it as me taking her side. But what could I do? She was my daughter, and I was deeply sorry. I can be deeply sorry and also understand how Emily's early life affected her. It is just so sad, because we have such a close family. I was a stay-at-home mom and would travel in the summers and spend a lot of time with my sister and her kids but this really put a wedge in our family. I was uninvited from my other niece's wedding because Hannah was afraid if she saw me or had to speak to me she would have PTSD. Honestly, I don't know if my family will ever be able to get over this. They really saw me as choosing Emily over Hannah, but I don't know what I could have done differently.

While my marriage struggled to survive with everything that was happening with Emily, it did not survive all that happened with my son, Chase. We later found out that he was sexually abused during the time he was placed back with his birth family. We found this out from his journals he wrote years later. We strongly suspect Emily was abused as well, but she doesn't have the same memory as Chase does. We were so naive when adopting these children. Even though we had to take months of required training before fostering our kids, we were totally unprepared for how their trauma would manifest into behaviors we didn't expect.

Chase would act up when he was little and touch my breasts, and display other odd behavior. We asked his therapist and she said to tell him it was inappropriate behavior and explain that we do not touch other people's privates. He understood and never did it again. When he hit puberty, he started trying to peek in on me when I was undressing. He even tried to videotape me when I took a shower. I'd have to lock the doors and check very carefully that the windows were locked. He would try to climb from the roof into the bathroom window. It got so bad that we didn't know what to do so he ended up in a psychiatric hospital for two weeks. After that, we had about six months of outpatient therapy where I would pick him up from school and drop him off to do three hours of therapy. It was very intense. Chase continued to get more and more aggressive. We ended up having to force him to go to a school for sexually deviant kids and a group therapy home. He wasn't able to be around me. They were afraid he was going to rape me. He had gotten so aggressive that he would try to break locks on doors. I was never afraid of Chase, but everyone in my life was very concerned that something might happen to me, my husband most of all. As sad as it is, he grew to hate him. While Chase was in the group home, only my husband could go see him, because they didn't want him seeing his "victim," me. I never thought of myself that way, but the school did. Most of the kids in the program had sexually abused a sister, or another relative, usually not a mother. Most were there because the police had gotten involved. Chase was there for two years. When he was a freshman in high school things started getting bad and my husband and I separated. There was an incident when I had caught Chase videotaping me again. My husband and I had begun intense couples therapy. Our therapist explained that if I wanted our marriage to work, I couldn't keep these things from my him, so I told him about the videotaping incident.

The reason I had not been telling my husband about everything was because he got very angry and had roughed Chase up once before. I was truly frightened he would hurt him again.

That night that it got bad, Emily and I were out running errands and Chase called me crying. He said, "Dad got home from work and beat me up." I came home and immediately took Chase out of the house to get him away from my husband. After my husband left, he said that I had picked Chase over him and we separated for about two months. He apologized to the whole family and asked to come back home and we tried to make things work.

When Chase finally came back from the group home, things seemed to be looking up. He had a great senior year! But the toll it had taken on my marriage was just too much and eventually, my marriage dissolved, and so did my relationship with Chase. He has severe ADHD and needs medication in order to manage life. He's currently homeless and still tries to break into our house. He's stolen my car, and there are drugs involved. Now, he self-medicates, mostly just with pot. It is very traumatic for all of us.

I've done a lot of therapy around this myself, and my therapist told me to think of it as an abusive relationship. In an abusive relationship, the abusive party never stops abusing. Similarly, in my relationship with Chase, the abuse isn't going to stop. Even though he is no longer sexually stalking me, he tries to break into the house and steal from us. Something in him doesn't respect me or see me as a person who he shouldn't take advantage of. There's nothing I can do or say to change it. I can't make him obey me, he's an adult. I can't reason with him or make him listen to me. It's such a difficult situation. My ex-husband is a good guy, he just couldn't handle all of this. The social worker who supported us through the adoption process became a friend. She's asked me before if I would like CPS to take the kids back, in light of everything that was going on at the time. She didn't mean it in a bad way, she truly saw how much I was struggling. But these were my kids. There's no giving them back. I truly did everything I could think of. I paid for the best therapists I could find, and the foster agency paid for additional therapy programs and group homes. I tried so hard, but it is so clear that sexual abuse from a young age can have severe lasting impacts. Of course, I wasn't always perfect. There are times I hit a breaking point. I wish I could say I never yelled at the kids or grabbed them by the arm and made a mark, but I did. We were under so much stress, so much pressure. But I truly did the best I could.

Emily is really upset with how she feels I've treated her brother. She feels like by cutting contact with him, I've given up on him. I've tried to explain to her that I can't be abused. I can't be in contact with someone who treats me this way. I don't think she understands the severity of his behavior towards me. I have so much compassion for both of them. When I first found out what Emily had done, I did feel a lot of anger. At the time, I didn't know that she had been sexually abused by Kelsey. I also think some of this anger came out of the embarrassment of having to tell those close to us who had children what she'd done. With Chase, compassion came easier. I think it was because, in this case, I was the victim. We were all victims in a way, my husband, my marriage, and Emily too. My husband used to get so upset that he wouldn't want to interact with Chase at all. He wouldn't want to hear whatever he'd done that day. But I was the direct victim. It made it strangely easier for me to try to understand why he was doing what he was doing. But eventually, I've come to hold the same compassion for both of them. Even when it's hard. Even though Chase cannot currently be part of my life.

I could not have made it through all this without my faith in God. I can't tell you how many times I walked around the block and just prayed and prayed and prayed and prayed and prayed. I also think medication helped, not just for the kids but also for me. I think it was my relationship with God that allowed me to continue to have compassion for them. I still love them, and have such deep compassion for them. I felt as though adopting them was a calling from God. I knew I was supposed to take these kids and because this calling came from God, I knew he would help me. And he did. Every step of the way. Every time I would be at my wits' end, God would have an answer for me. Like if Emily was really struggling at school, a teacher would go out of their way to help me. Or once, when we thought Chase was bipolar, we went to get him diagnosed. He hadn't ever had a manic episode before, but had been very moody and we were trying to figure out what kinds of medications he needed. The day we went into the psychologist's office he began experiencing mania, rolling on the floor, feeling elated but in an unstable way. Because the doctor was able to see what was happening with him, we were able to get the meds he needed and confirm he was probably bipolar. It was a miracle that it happened when it did. We were able to help him, at least for a little while. God came through for us. I remember shortly after what happened with Emily, a friend of mine hosted Bible Study at her house. It was usually at my house, but I couldn't because of everything that was going on that day and I missed the session. After she hosted, my friend came over and sat with me and read the story that they'd gone over in Bible Study. It was about the idea of gentleness. And after we read the story, she sat with me and we talked about how gentleness is all about acceptance. It was exactly what I needed. She came the next day and sat with me again. There were so many people who God worked through, so many people who supported me. Even though there were losses along the way, my marriage, my relationship with Chase, I am so thankful for adopting Chase and Emily for the blessing and lessons I have learned. The biggest blessing was having my son Parker. After trying to get pregnant for eight years, I immediately got pregnant right after adopting Emily and Chase. I remember telling God I thought he was very funny for giving me three kids in one year. My husband and I always call Parker the blessing baby. We adopted the kids and God blessed us with a baby. Parker was best friends with Chase for years. Most kids would not want their younger brother hanging out with them all the time, but Chase thought nothing of taking Parker with him to his friends' houses and to the park with him and everywhere else he went. Even when Chase was in high school he would stay home with Parker to watch their favorite shows together. Once when he was little, I explained to Parker that if we had not adopted Emily and Chase, he would be an only child. He looked at me and said, "That is not a real family." Parker has been there through all the ups and downs his siblings experienced, and it has made him exceptionally empathetic, compassionate and kind.

Emily and Chase both have great hearts and I know they are in God's hands. Like all of us, they're a work in progress. And so am I. I am constantly being stretched to become a more loving, compassionate person. My experiences raising my children have given me a greater ability to love and an unwavering faith.

PART 4

I DESERVE
SUPPORT

"You don't have to do this alone. There are resources to help and support you. Somebody always has the answer so be strong and look for them."

—My prayer for you

CHAPTER 12

HEALING FROM CHILDHOOD SEXUAL ABUSE

"You can be healthy, you can be happy, and you absolutely can heal."

Jaime Calle is a licensed marriage and family therapist. He has been practicing for thirty-six years and has several specializations including forensic mental health, rapid resolution therapy and EMDR.

He felt it was very important to help to get this book into the world. It is so important to clear the shame from childhood sexual trauma so that survivors can heal and live fulfilled, functional lives. —Jill E. Schultz

When we speak of those who acted out as children due to having been sexually abused themselves, it is important to note that these children who act out are not pedophiles. A pedophile is defined as an adult who is sexually attracted to children. Often the developmental age of a child who has been sexually abused is much younger than their actual age. A twelve-year-old who is sexually abusing another child may have the maturity and intellectual level of a child who is much younger. The majority of the time, when children are acting out, they are doing something that somebody did to them or showed them how to do. It can be incredibly difficult for a child to interpret that what was done to them was inappropriate, especially if, physically, it felt good. So when children engage in sexually abusing other children, they are not thinking in terms of abuse. They are simply acting out.

This can be especially exacerbated when a child has been groomed. In a positive developmental situation, children learn that if they do something good then they get a reward. A little girl might learn, "If I do well in school, then I get to go for ice cream or pizza." When children are groomed, they learn that if they tolerate or participate in a sexual act with an adult, something positive will happen. They get to go to the movies or to the park, or they get praise or approval from the person who is abusing them. This can, of course, create a lot of confusion for these children, both during their childhoods and into adulthood. They feel guilty as though they participated in their abuse, even though they were coerced. They feel shame because they now know that what they did to other children was wrong, even though when they were taught to behave this way they were rewarded.

This guilt and shame often leads to difficulty in adulthood— whether it be issues of addiction, mood disorders, self-harm, or eating disorders. These symptoms don't always point to a history of sexual abuse. Of course people can experience any number of these things without having been sexually abused, but there is often a connection. Sometimes these disorders are about control.

When people feel out of control, using what you put in your body or do with your body to numb the bad feelings can become a coping mechanism, whether the addictive substance is a drug, or sex, or food. Restrictive eating and self-harming often come from this feeling of "Well, I can't control what's happened to me, but I can control this." This isn't always conscious. Again, those exhibiting these behaviors might not have a history of sexual abuse, but when this history is present, many of these behaviors may arise during adolescence or adulthood.

One of the questions that so often comes up around the sexual abuse of children is, "How do I protect my child, or the children in my life?" It is not by attempting to supervise them twenty-four hours a day. That simply isn't possible. Additionally, when children are molested, over 90% of the time the perpetrator is someone they know—someone within the family, or a friend of the family—rather than a stranger. People often say, "I am going to put my kids in karate or Taekwondo so they can fight off an abuser." That's great for exercise and for learning discipline, but it isn't useful as a preventative measure against sexual abuse. What is truly helpful is to teach children about behaviors they might encounter from adults that aren't appropriate. It's important to teach children about grooming. Pedophiles almost always groom children. There's an idea that pedophiles are bad guys who lurk behind bushes waiting to jump out and grab a child. This is extremely rare. What is extremely common is grooming.

For example, a pedophile might say to a child, "You have really beautiful hair. Let me brush your hair." The pedophile might have the child sit on his or her lap so that he or she can brush the child's hair. So far, nothing is wrong. It is normal for an adult to brush a child's hair. But for a pedophile, this accomplishes four important goals. 1. The child gets used to sitting in his or her lap. 2. The child gets used to his or her touch. 3. If anyone else walks into the room, it's fine. Nothing seems to be amiss. 4. The perpetrator gets sexually stimulated from it. Often, during the first little step, there isn't anything obviously wrong. To the child and to the outside world, it seems normal, but it is one step closer to what the pedophile actually wants.

Another example would be a coach who might offer to drive a child home after practice or a game. When he has the child alone in the car, he drops something, perhaps his keys, and swears. He turns to the child and says, "Please don't tell your mom and dad I swore, or I will get in trouble. This is our secret." If the pedophile doesn't hear from that child's parents, he knows the child kept the secret. He knows that if he does victimize this child, the child is less likely to tell and he is less likely to get caught.

Circumstances of Childhood Sexual Abuse

Statistics regarding child sexual abuse in USA vary depending on the source. These variations can be easily explained by the differences in the collection of information, geographical circumstances and state regulations. Organizations like the CDC, the National Center for Victims of Crime, the Office of Child Abuse Prevention, and the National Child Abuse Coalition provide general statistics as reference points. All statistics demonstrate that, in general, 1 out of 4 girls and 1 out of 7 boys are molested each year, throughout the country. Also, on average, 91% of the abusers are persons who are related, known and/ or trusted by the child and his/her parents. It is important to emphasize here that these numbers only reflect the cases that are reported, and not the actual number of incidents. It is generally believed that in the majority of the cases, the parents of children who experience abuse do not report the situation to the law or to any official organization. At the same time, it is necessary to consider the numbers on the other side of the coin. The amount of registered sex offenders has, statistically, grown steadily in the USA during the last ten years. In the state of California there are currently 104,000 registered sex offenders. As with the statistics on the victims, this number of registered sex offenders only shows those people who were caught, so the number does not reflect the reality of the situation. Another very important fact to be considered is that the general population does not have clear knowledge of what constitutes sexual abuse. Some people even recall inappropriate circumstances during their childhood but make statements like, "I was lucky that nobody molested me," simply because there was not an actual penetration. Child sexual abuse does not require penetration, and inappropriate circumstances can create as much emotional trauma as those where penetration occurred. Here is a list of activities that are sexual abuse, with both penetration and no penetration:

With penetration:

– Intercourse
– Anal sex
– Oral sex with the victim's mouth being penetrated
– Penetration with fingers and/or objects

Without penetration:

– Fondling
– Making the victim fondle the perpetrator

- Exposing the victim to pornographic materials
- Exposing the victim to sexual activities
- Taking pictures/videos of victims in "sexy" postures and activities
- Performing oral sex
- Verbalizing sexual comments to a child about his/her body

How to Protect Your Child from Being Abused

In order to protect a child, you have to give the child information. The older method of trying to keep children safe was teaching them about "Stranger Danger." This doesn't work, because so often the pedophile isn't a stranger. People in therapy often describe situations where they didn't tell someone who could help them about the abuse because they'd been taught to never talk to strangers. Instead of putting the fear of Stranger Danger in a child's mind, give the child information that is actually useful.

It's important to keep in mind that discussions with children around adults who behave inappropriately aren't to be presented as "The Talk." You need to have hundreds and hundreds of talks. People have it in their heads that these talks are difficult, frightening or embarrassing, and might only happen once. A parent sits you down and tells you about "the birds and the bees." This is absurd—what else do you learn by only talking about it one time? A child cannot learn subtraction, for example, by only talking about it once. These conversations are the same. You talk about it over and over, and as the child grows the level of detail and nuance grows with them. When children are very young, these conversations should be as simple as possible and relevant to their level of understanding and maturity. As they get older, they will ask more complex questions that require more complex answers.

People often ask at what age a child should stop bathing with a parent. A sign that a child is ready to begin learning about private parts and bathing separately is when they begin to notice and ask questions about different parts of the parent's body, and notice that their own body is very different from their parent's. Of course a child is always going to ask questions. If they don't know what something is, they're going to ask about it. A sign that a child is ready to begin learning about privacy is when they begin to compare themselves to a parent, like, "How come you have that and I don't?" Or, "Why do you have hair there?" This is a good developmental sign that it is time to start to build the idea of privacy for your child.

Exploration of body parts is a normal process in the development of children. Shaming and punishing them for exploring can teach them that their private parts are dirty or bad. When we talk about them as special, the child can develop a healthy sense of privacy without developing that shame.

Signs a Child Is Being Abused

It is also important to be aware of behaviors that might indicate a child in your life is being sexually abused. There are many behaviors that could be signs and it is very, very important to understand that one sign doesn't mean anything unless it is a clear sign of abuse. Three or more signs clearly demonstrate that there is something going on. While we often look to see a child exhibiting at least three of these signs, some of these examples are severe enough that they would still be an indication to seek help. The following are signs of child sexual abuse.

Unexplained sexual knowledge. The clearest sign of all is when a child has sexual knowledge that cannot be explained by what the parents have told the child. Here are two examples. When a little girl thinks of her vagina and how she uses it, she thinks about it as going to pee. There was a case in which a little girl came home with a crayon and asked her mother if she wanted to see a magic trick she'd learned. The mother said, "Of course!" The child then stuck the crayon in her vagina. There's no way this little girl came up with that on her own. She wouldn't know that things could go inside her vagina unless someone either showed her or did it to her.

Another example that comes to mind is the time a little boy during a therapy session said he wanted to draw. He wanted to draw a woman. The therapist started drawing her face and the little boy said, "Who cares about the face, I just want a nice set of tits and a juicy pussy." Now, this boy was seven years old. This is not language he should know at this point. It was eventually discovered that his mother had been exchanging sex for drugs, and often this child was in the bed while that occurred.

Potty Training Regression. This is when a child, after having been potty trained, goes back to having accidents. *Enuresis* is the term for urination accidents; *encopresis* means accidents involving defecation. It is important to remember that one incident of wetting or soiling clothes or bedding may not mean anything, but repeated accidents in a child who was previously potty trained are a potential sign of abuse.

Unexplained or sudden fear of people or places. An example would be a child who used to love to go to the park and suddenly becomes frightened to go or refuses to do so, or a child who used to love visiting grandpa but no longer wants to see him or begs not to have to go.

Children who engage in sexual acts. If a little girl suddenly pulls down the pants of the child in front of her, or a little boy takes his penis out in the classroom, or if a child is asking other children to touch his or her private parts, this can be a sign that the child has been abused.

How to React If You Find Out Your Child Has Been Hurt

Even children who have been given all the information to help keep themselves safe can still end up being sexually molested. How parents react when they find out their child has been molested is extremely important. Many parents experience so much guilt and shame around their child's disclosure that they go into denial. They say, "That must not have happened," or they ignore it, because they blame themselves for not being able to protect their child. It's also important not to overreact and say things like, "I'm going to kill him." This can actually prevent a child from speaking up, or make them feel guilty for having told. They can end up feeling very responsible for any negative consequences that occur because they told someone what happened. If you find out your child has been molested, one of the first things to do is to seek proper therapy. Make sure the therapist specializes in this area, specializes in working with children, and that he or she has actual experience working with children who have been sexually abused. Ask lots of questions in your initial consultation. Make sure they're familiar with the laws around child abuse, that they're familiar with Child Protective Services and their protocols and processes. It is important to find a therapist, but especially important to find the right therapist, one who has the necessary experience and with whom your child feels comfortable.

Explain to the child why they're going to see a therapist. Explain that this person is someone they can trust, and they can talk about anything they need to talk about. In these conversations, it is important to remain calm. It is also important to explain to the child that the adult who molested them did something wrong, but the child didn't do anything wrong. They were misled, and it was not their fault. It is the pedophile's fault because they did something wrong and they *knew* what they were doing was wrong. Be as calm and as gentle as possible. Keep emphasizing that they did nothing wrong, they were misled, and so it isn't his or her fault. So many people who were abused as children end up with so much guilt as adults. The clearer you are that the child has nothing to be ashamed of or to feel guilty about, the better. Ask them if they have questions. Keep the conversation going. The more the child can talk about what happened and process without shame, the better off they'll be as an adult.

If you have a friend who is struggling due to a history of childhood sexual abuse, it is an honorable thing to want to be there to support him or her. First, however, you need to consider if they're actually asking for help. Many people will say, "I'm going to help you!" This is a good impulse, but people who are not asking for help will never be open to receiving it. Often, the best course of action is to ask, "What do you need or want from me at this moment? I want to help you." If they don't know or aren't able to articulate what they want, ask if you can offer suggestions. Empower people by honoring what they want. It is often better to give them a couple of names and numbers of therapists, rather than to make the appointment for them. Stepping in and making the appointment for them is disempowering, unless they specifically say, "Hey, will you help me set up an appointment? I haven't been able to do it." Then it would be appropriate to help in that way. *Keep in mind that unless you actually are their therapist, you're not their therapist.* Encourage them to get professional support. Go slow, be kind.

If you were abused as a child, be aware the memories are often foggy and traumatic. The truth is, you don't need more insight about what happened. When you are trying to heal from a history of sexual abuse, it is most helpful to look at the circumstances of your life now. Are you struggling with boundaries and saying yes to things you want to say no to? Do you struggle with social bonds and find yourself disconnected from your friends and family? Do you struggle with depression, with your sex life and intimate partners? Do you have low self-esteem? Those are signs that your mind and your body are telling you something needs to be taken care of. These are signs to seek therapeutic help.

You can achieve the healthy, joyful life that you deserve even though you experienced sexual abuse. It is possible to look at your life and say, "Yeah, I've got some weird and uncomfortable memories, but my life functions well. I'm really good at setting boundaries. I have good, nourishing friendships. I seek intimate relationships with healthy people. I really feel good about myself." This is completely possible for you. You can be healthy, you can be happy, and you absolutely can heal.

PART 5

I GET TO THRIVE

"It is my hope that you decide right now that your shame no longer has power over you. You get to love yourself, you get to heal, you get to forgive, and you get to live the life of your dreams."

—My prayer for you

CHAPTER 13

SARA

*"I needed a lot of healing, and it was hard.
But at some point I decided that I get to have this
absolutely amazing life. You get to decide that too.
Healing is worth it.
That's where all the magic is waiting."*

I'm forty-seven. I'm so honored to have this conversation and to be speaking into the idea that we can have experiences that feel unhealable and devastating, but the wholeness inside of us maintains itself. No matter what experiences we've had, we actually can create a phenomenal life. So I'm starting at the end, where I am still whole, where I am happy, and where I *have* a phenomenal life. Then, I'll rewind. I really don't believe in revenge, but I do love the phrase, "the best revenge is wild success." To me success is happiness, well-being, and the ability to receive abundance and share abundance, and to be visible in the world and share our gifts and talents. Success is doing what we're called to do and what we love. And I'm doing that. That's the end, and that's why I want to start there. I'm proof that it's possible.

Now here's the rewind. I was raised in a devout Catholic family. My dad almost was a priest in the seminary before he decided to have a family. We were middle class, at times lower middle class.

I always felt like the one that didn't belong. The ugly duckling narrative is very much a story and an archetype that I relate to, in the sense that I felt my parents adored my two younger sisters and I felt as though I was a problem. The irony is that because of that environment, I desperately wanted achievement and positive affirmation so I became an A student, and I did athletics, was captain of varsity teams, got the lead in plays. I tried to do everything right.

The problem, it seemed, is that I was an intense kid. Highly sensitive. To my family, I was always "too much." Honestly, I'm still intense. I feel things deeply, I express really big emotions. My mother is an introvert, and could not tolerate all those feelings, all the big dreaming. My way of being was triggering. There was this constant feeling of "You're too intense, you're too dramatic, you have too many feelings. You're too much of *everything*." My sisters were quieter. They were easier. One Christmas I actually got so excited I threw up, and was mocked for years. When I asked for things I was treated in a way that I interpreted as my being selfish or greedy. The message I received was that I should be able to control myself and my emotions. None of this should have been a big deal but it set up an experience of me feeling very alone and wrong. (I know now this isolation and worthlessness feeling can be a setup for attracting trauma.)

The first incident that happened, in terms of sexual abuse, was with two boys that were a few years older than I was at the time. I was around six years old, and the older one was probably ten and the younger around eight or nine. They came over to my house and we were playing in the basement. The older boy started to tell me and the younger boy to do things to each other. Like, "Sara, take off your shirt. Johnny, touch Sara's chest." I had no idea what was going on. I was six years old. I knew nothing about what sex was, or what these actions might relate to or mean. But I knew that I was scared. I knew I did not like the game. I didn't like what was going on. I tried to leave and the older boy blocked the door.

He pulled down his pants and told me to put my hand on his penis. He didn't call it a penis, he called it something strange like a runway or something. And I said "No." Then the other boy kind of held me and grabbed my hand and forced me to touch him. A visercal shock went through my body. I knew something had just happened and that it was bad. This is really interesting in hindsight, because of what science has proven about cellular memory. Something was imprinted, something had changed. Eventually, he had us laying on each other and moving up and down. And again, I didn't have any context. But I knew something felt off, felt scary. Eventually I said no again, and that I was going to yell for my mom. I remember them threatening me. He told me about a girl in our neighborhood who we used to see a lot and then hadn't in months. He said she told after they did something like this and she was taken away from her family. She disappeared. I remember feeling terrified. This deep sense of terror and shame.

This kid scared me. He had a bullying energy. Even in other capacities, even when we played with a larger group of friends, he was a bully. I left the experience in the basement shivering. I'd sweated through my t-shirt. I remember shaking for hours, desperately wanting to tell my mother what happened. But I didn't want to be taken from my family. I never told anyone.

I look back on this now and wonder what was going on in his home? Who had taught him this behavior? No kid makes this up. Years later, when I told my father about the experience he said, "I never trusted that kid."

Two years later, I was sleeping over at a friend's house. She and I went to the same school, and we were eight years old, in the third grade. I'd met her mother but she wasn't home. My friend's father was there, with his girlfriend. The dad and his girlfriend were kind of stumbling around. At the time, I didn't know what being drunk was because my parents weren't drinkers, but I now understand that he was trashed. This friend and I took dance classes together, and he said, "Oh, do a dance for us." The request gave me an odd feeling. And then he told us to take our shirts off. I remember being confused. I was wearing some sort of one-piece, like a leotard or a bathing suit, so I couldn't really take off my top. Eventually, I went to the bathroom. He was waiting for me when I came out. He kind of used his body to move me into the bedroom, and he shut the door behind him. He said, "I'm going to show you what grownups do."

My memory goes pretty foggy after that until I remember the same sense of shaking I'd felt in my basement. I do have enough body memories after extensive therapy that point to rape, though honestly it doesn't matter if it was molestation or a rape; it was an assault. As he walked me out of his room, he told me that if I told anyone he would find out and kill my family. I walked silently to my friend's room and pushed the bureau against the door. Again, I never said a word.

After I changed from Catholic school to public school in my neighborhood, I didn't see that friend again until a week before I left for college. I ran into her at a party; I think it was a party for people who had been lifeguards that summer. When I saw her, I went numb. Then the shaking started. I heard her bragging about visiting the university where she was going and how she'd slept with a whole group of lacrosse players during her school visit.

Years later when I finally acknowledged what had happened and more fully remembered the incident, I remember realizing: "Oh my god, he was doing that to her too."

It was really heartbreaking, but also weirdly validating to understand IT HAD HAPPENED. I knew it in my cells. I also understood she'd had sex with an entire lacrosse team because she wanted to feel powerful. She wanted to CHOOSE to act vs. continuing to be a victim.

These were my two primary childhood experiences with sexual abuse. In high school, there were these classic high-school bullies who did a lot of sexual bullying. I don't think this sort of thing is talked about that much. You hear a lot about sexual abuse, but there's so much sexual bullying that happens. The three boys in our school ran as a pack. They would put hands down girls' shirts, grope our butts, sometimes fully in front of teachers. No one did anything about it. After one of the boys licked my face on stage during a rehearsal for Hamlet, the drama teacher said, "Boys, stop messing around." I sat there as if I were paralyzed. I could not pull away once this behavior started. I froze every time. One day during a tech rehearsal, the three of them dragged me into a storage room. Somehow, they'd found out that I hadn't slept with my boyfriend, that I was a virgin (I didn't let myself remember all that happened in third grade—I really thought I was!). I had a really nice boyfriend. I was so afraid of sex, which of course, now

I understand why. He was patient and lovely. But somehow, these bullies found out we hadn't had sex, so they dragged me into this room and said, "We're gonna rape you."

I ended up getting away. They were huge, but I screamed, and I fought. I don't know if they were fully intending on carrying through with raping me in that room in the school, but it was terrifying. I told a teacher and she said, "Well, no one saw it." I also told a guidance counselor. He shrugged. We didn't have any proof. Eventually, I demanded to be transferred out of drama.

The last experience I'll share happened when I got my first job right after college. I went to work at an advertising agency in Chicago. It was right out of Me Too. It was every single cliché about male-dominated industries. Young women were prey. We were expected to accompany clients to strip clubs. I experienced many assaults, verbal and physical. One night, I was working late. I got a call from within the office. It was this group of guys who worked there, and they pretended they were asking about my boyfriend at the time (the man who is now my husband). They said they were doing some kind of game—like "how well do you know your boyfriend" and were calling each other's girlfriends to get the answers. The winner would win a bottle of champagne. It seemed odd but I started answering: my favorite vacation spot, favorite food, best book but then the questions became sexual. It was so strange, because I knew Bill would never participate in something like this but again I froze. I couldn't make my hand hang up the phone. Then I heard grunting and a slapping sound and I realized the men were jerking off. My head swam with all the noises, and grunting. I went to human resources the next morning to file a complaint. They said they couldn't trace it because it was an internal call. There was apparently nothing they could do.

I tell this story to show how there ended up being a pattern. I would be in a situation where the authority figures were either absent, unaware or totally unwilling to do anything to help me, and these scenarios of abuse kept repeating. I can see this pattern so clearly. It's hard to talk about this sort of thing without sounding like I am blaming my younger self. I'm not. But there's a pattern of this victim/ perpetrator energy and dynamic. I think I basically sent out a signal that said, "I'm not going to tell. I'm not going to talk."

I don't want to suggest blame or responsibility for anyone else in their victimization, but in my own healing it has actually felt empowering to see that there's a pattern that got set, and that once I saw it, I was able to break that pattern. I realized until I was able to break the pattern, it would likely keep happening. I was thankfully able to leave that job, and to do the healing work around the trauma I was carrying. The experience of not speaking out, not telling anyone, and being silenced the few times I did try to advocate for myself in high school and at that agency left me feeling broken. I just felt despair. I felt powerless. Breaking this pattern has been a way to get my power back.

This work hasn't been easy. Leaving that job was the start of the healing journey I'm still on today. That job was my breaking point. But healing didn't come fast. I developed an eating disorder as a result of not knowing how to process the trauma. There are statistics that say, if you have a childhood sexual trauma, you have a 98% chance of developing an addiction of some kind. Mine was food. It could have been drugs or alcohol. Food was the one I chose. It was, like with all addictions, progressive, and it was becoming increasingly dangerous. I was binging and starving myself in extremes.

Starving was my form of cutting. I've heard people say that they can't imagine ever cutting, but I've always understood. Starving was how I could control the pain. I felt as though if I didn't have any needs, I wouldn't feel anything. It was a great anesthetizer. It was an effective drug for me for a long time. Until it started to kill me.

When I finally felt a desire to heal I didn't know where to turn. I stopped being able to sleep, which was horrible. Sleep was my only escape from wanting food, and from having what I now understand were PTSD flashbacks. One night I actually fell to the ground. "I can't go on. I can't go on like this. I can't keep this job. I can't keep doing this with food." I knew something was very wrong. I didn't understand food as an addiction or any of this at that point, but this sort of presence came into the room and I could almost hear it say, "You will sleep when you deal with your pain."

I ended up going to a doctor who prescribed me sleeping pills. As I left the office I knew in my heart that if I went down that road there was no coming back. I think this is why I never did drugs and I didn't drink much. I think I knew if I started I would never come back. But what I was doing with food was just like what a drug addict does with drugs. To have any hope of healing, I needed sobriety. I started a twelve-step program called Overeaters Anonymous. I know some people have lots of conflicting feelings about twelve-step programs, but it was a powerful lifeline for me. It was loving and healing, and I was able to get stability. I was able to go to a doctor and a nutritionist. I started eating actual meals. I was able to get my health back. I still go to some Overeaters Anonymous meetings. You can even go on Zoom. I now know there's an alternative to self-harm with food—that there are better ways to let go of the pain.

If you are struggling with food addictions or disorders, click or scan here to access the Resource Center at my website and find help. —Jill E. Schultz

Resource Center at <u>www.jilleschultz.com/gethelp</u>

Or, please go to the Resources Section on page 179 to find help.

Right at the start of my food recovery, I moved to London. For the first time, I was an ocean away from where my trauma took place, and I was able to have the privacy to heal.

In London, I started working with a therapist. I started to do work around the patterns I'd learned in my family. I confessed that since I achieved a healthier relationship with food, I had stopped being able to have sex. "It's like I see my husband as an attacker. Something is very wrong with me." She referred me to a whole bunch of specialists around England. My husband and I went to a marriage counselor where I shared I could only have sex if I used alcohol. But I had stopped drinking any alcohol as I healed my food addiction. Fully present, I shut down. I went into a regressed state.

I went for my first acupuncture treatment on the recommendation of the therapist and that's where I learned about cellular memory. The needles went in and there, like watching a movie, the memories came flooding back. Memories from when I was six, from when I was eight, from when I was a teenager. My friend's father reaching for me in that bedroom. "I'm going to show you what grownups do."

I was sick for an entire week. Vomiting, diarrhea, sweating, fever. I told my husband I had the flu, because I didn't know how to tell him what I was experiencing. I thought I was going insane. But part of me did know it was real, and that I was remembering. And I had all the signs of sexual abuse having happened, and all the memories around it. My body felt like a fist that had been clutched tight for so long it hurt to open. I kept seeking help. I worked with shamans, I went to hypnosis, I went to sound healings, goddess workshops, tantric classes, meditation weekends, nature retreats. I tried being vegetarian and vegan. I tried craniosacral therapy, chiropractic, reflexology, reiki, psychic readings. I went to anyone who said they could help.

Of course, this was all really hard on my husband and on my marriage. My husband's number one love language is physical touch. We were newlyweds when all of this happened. I developed vaginismus, a condition where my vagina would tighten and intercourse was extremely painful. I ended up seeing a sex therapist from the Catholic church who prescribed me exercise with dilators, where you start with a very small phallus the size of a lipstick case and work your way up. It was clinical and so retraumatizing. I was in PTSD every single day trying to use them.

We eventually moved back to the US, and still nothing was budging as far as my ability to have sex. I would kind of grit my teeth and hold my breath and "get through it" once a month, but it was horrible for both of us. My husband tried to be understanding but he was confused and upset. He questioned if I was attracted to him. He wondered aloud, "Where did my wife go?" He didn't want to just be best friends, he wanted a complete relationship and so did I. A partner and a sexual partner. We saw yet another marriage counselor and I basically went there assuming we needed to get divorced. I didn't want to put him through any more of this. I didn't think I could ever get better.

A strange thing happened when we went to see this counselor. I was thinking this was the end, but she said, "No, I don't see that. I think you guys are meant to be together." And honestly, I was pissed. I didn't want to keep doing this work. I didn't want to keep feeling broken and defective. I didn't ever want to have sex again. I told her, I'd rather go have a root canal. I would rather be waterboarded than have sex. I meant it. I loved my husband. I was attracted to him. I just couldn't stop being eight years old in that bedroom. I was Ophelia underwater, drowned. I felt cursed.

It's crazy that we stayed together. We laugh about it now because I asked him why he stayed. And he said, "I know who you are. I knew if you decided to heal this, you were going to heal it. Whatever it took." At that time, I didn't believe that about myself, but he said he knew in his gut that I was going to. It was almost a decade of this. We were both in pain for a really long time.

Then I began hearing wild stories about a certain therapist. That he was a Yale psychiatrist. That he was into exposure therapy (a therapy where you face exactly what you are afraid of and cure yourself by confronting the fear head on.) A woman I knew whispered, "He runs an incest group."

Something in my body jumped. I was terrified, but I'd heard that there were people who worked with him that couldn't have sex and then, suddenly, they could. I thought about the group for months. Finally, I reached out and he told me that he had one available spot. He asked me, "Are you going to do the work?" And I didn't know. I didn't know what the work was. Did we have sex in front of him for "exposure"? Was it a cult? Would that count as cheating if it was therapy?

He answered none of these questions. I joined the group and decided, cult or not, I would do whatever was suggested. I'd exhausted every modality I could find on earth. I showed up every Wednesday. The work was bizarre. Confrontational. Some weeks we screamed or hit a padded block with a nerf bat. I started doing a twelve-step program around sexual abuse. There's one called SIA, Survivors of Incest Anonymous.

If you are a survivor of incest, click or scan here to access the Resource Center at my website. SIAWSO is listed there, along with other resources. —Jill E. Schultz

Resource Center at www.jilleschultz.com/gethelp

Or, please go to the Resources Center on page 179 to get help.

It's not just incest as in abuse within the family, it's for anyone who has experienced childhood sexual abuse and trauma. Because it helped so much around the body and food stuff, I was so hopeful that this twelve-step program would help with the sexual abuse I was processing. I worked with that therapist and went to SIA for about six years.

It didn't happen instantly, but eventually I was able to start showing up as a more consistent sexual partner, first and foremost with myself and then with my husband. We've now been married for twenty-one years. It's been a wild journey. There's so much talk about sex in society, in movies, people making jokes about it, and I had this feeling of deepest, deepest shame because I couldn't do it. Being in that level of PTSD and trauma is so lonely. I think the group I worked with was such a gift because EVERYTHING was discussed there. There were so many stories of people who were abused as children who acted out with other children, with siblings, with cousins, sexual assaults they experienced as adults. For the first time, I did not feel alone. I released decades of shame and body pain. My husband and I joke we should erect a bust of my therapist in our home. We have his unusual work to thank for the really, really good sex life we have today. I count this as a miracle of my lifetime. Something I was certain could never be healed, has been healed. We joke about the narrative that most people will have a good sex life at the beginning of the marriage, and then they'll get older and have kids and life dampens the flame. I think that's actually bullshit—we can create great sex at any age and any duration of relationship. And for us, sex has gotten better the longer we've been together.

Struggling with it really made us value it. We prioritize it. It's sacred. We have regular sex dates as a practice in our marriage.

Of course, I can still get triggered. Even after all of this work, there's still pieces to navigate. I went to a friend's wedding a few years ago, and one of those high school bullies that pulled me into the storage room was there. I went into a kind of shock. That same shaking. I don't remember any of the rest of the night even though I wasn't drinking. The next day though, new feelings washed over me. What had been happening to those three boys that they would act the way they did? Who had done the same thing to them?

I do feel sad that my abuse experiences were such a huge factor in my life, and the trauma took so long to heal. But I don't wish ill to any of the people that hurt me. Yes, they're accountable for their actions. Yes, I certainly feel very upset that it happened, and I don't wish it on anyone ever. But I don't hate them. I don't carry resentment. No one violates a child who is feeling healthy and well.

I especially see the boys in the basement as other victims. My son is eleven now, and he still seems so young. So kind. Innocent. The boys that acted out on me that day were recreating something they'd seen—something they'd been taught.

So I go back to what I shared earlier. The best "revenge" against the past pain is living a wildly happy and successful life now!

I want to tell every one of you reading this that yes, you have suffered. You've suffered enough for lifetimes. It's over. You don't have to continue to suffer. Those of us who have had childhood sexual abuse often suffer in other areas due to the abuse. One of these, for me, was financially. I had a difficult time earning money. I learned in my studies that the sacral chakra governs sexuality and money. During my healing I realized how connected my trauma around sexuality and my difficulty with money really were. If I could fund a study, I would love to see some solid research on a connection between earning and childhood sexual abuse, the same way there have been studies about addiction and childhood sexual abuse. There was a connection of difficulty there for me, and I do think others may have experienced this. If you've struggled to create abundance for yourself, I want to stand here and show that that healing is possible as well.

After I began healing sexually, I became really clear about my life's work. I was coaching, I was writing, I was doing all the things I wanted to do but I could not make money. It was blocked, just like how sex had been blocked for me. I took on the work of creating abundance in the exact same way I took on the work of sexual healing. It was an immersion. I was going to live it and sleep it and breathe it, do meditations, go to healers. Last year, my company had its first seven-figure year, and this year we crossed two million in sales. We've been doubling every year. I want to speak into this because just as the sexual abuse had left me feeling broken and hopeless around sex, it left me feeling broken and hopeless around money. Knowing now that they're energetically related and housed in the same chakra makes so much sense.

Success is possible for you. A beautiful relationship is possible for you. My husband and I walked through fire together. I do think relationships can be healing journeys. My husband had a lot of childhood trauma as well, involving physical abuse. We've been able to support each other through healing. It has been hard. We went through absolute hell getting pregnant and having a child. Again, I believe that was completely related. With all the trauma I experienced, I'm not surprised that my body struggled to conceive. It was really hard and painful, but I'm not surprised. But now we have this eleven-year-old boy, and he's an absolute force of nature and came into our lives in a miraculous way. I had always wanted a big family, but now I think it is a blessing that I can be a present mother and a present partner to my husband, as well as being called to my vocation.

I have my wonderful husband, and my son, and this year we bought a new house. It has a turret and huge canvases of modern art on the walls and it's magical and safe. I get to do the work that I value so much. I get to serve over a hundred clients a year and help them bring powerful, world-changing thought leadership to fruition. I'm writing my eighth book. Last week, I got to do a reading of my latest book in New York at my favorite bookstore and see billboards of the book in Times Square. I'm living my wildest dreams. Like you now, I'm the shero, not the victim.

Yes, shitty things happened to me, but it's not who I am. Trauma doesn't get to define me anymore. I think of a scene from *Lord of the Rings* sometimes. At a certain point, all of the hobbits and elves and dwarves (the little guys) are getting besieged by these giant, horrifying orcs and trolls. Gandalf, the wizard, takes his giant staff and plunges it into the ground. A shard of electric light forms a wall. He commands across the chasm, "You shall not pass!" And the monsters get blown back by this force field. We get to do that now. We get to say to those limiting ideas and memories and tormentors in our own heads, "You cannot pass here anymore. You don't get to own me, you don't get to have power over me now." I needed a lot of help to let that be real. I needed a lot of healing, and it was hard. But at some point I decided that I got to have this absolutely amazing life. You get to decide that, too. Healing is worth it. That's where all the magic is waiting.

PART 6

I GET TO HAVE IT ALL

*"Now that I have taken the time to look at the hard
things and do the work to heal, I know that I deserve
to have every desire that is in my heart. I hope that you
understand with every fiber in your being that you deserve
the same."*

—*My prayer for you*

CHAPTER 14

GLADYS

"What kind of God would put something in your heart, dangle it like a carrot in front of you, and not allow you to have it?"

When I decided to write this book, I had many reasons for doing so. 1. God was being very insistent that I speak out. 2. I felt this sudden sense of freedom because I had finally broken free from the self-loathing and shame and I wanted to share my path with anyone and everyone who was like me. 3. I had been holding myself back from love and success for years because I didn't feel I deserved them. I met Gladys when I was doing a lot of the work around my shame and she was pivotal in my breakthrough around self-love. I am on the path to calling in my soulmate and I wanted Gladys to share her story and how she created such an amazing relationship so if this is you, you also get to have that love in your life. Here is her story.

—Jill Schultz

It's easy for people to think that because of a background of abuse, abandonment, mental illness and addiction, they haven't been able to attract the right person. That's why they struggle to find the kind of love they want. My sister Michelle and I, a.k.a. The Love Twins can relate. We have similar histories, similar pathologies in our own family. When I was very young, my birth father and my grandfather died. My mother divorced my first stepfather, and then married my second stepfather who physically abused her. There was a huge layer of secrets and shame due to this abuse. *Nobody* could know about it. Eventually, my mom also left us. The cycle of abuse, addiction, and abandonment was repeated in yet another generation, and Michelle and I, along with our younger sister, were left feeling confused, abandoned, and unloved. Because, honestly, if your mom doesn't love you enough to stay, who will?

As a young adult, I did a lot of inner work to heal from these experiences. I had my first transformation at age seventeen. I reconnected with a friend I'd known since high school, had this beautiful love story, got married, and then he died in my arms. And I had this strong belief that I would never love or be loved again. If you talked to me at that time, at some point in that conversation, I would declare to you that I was a widow at twenty-seven, and I would never love or be loved again. One day I heard myself say it, and paused. I asked myself, "Wait, what did you just say?" And then I asked myself the question that changed my life: "*What* would have you say that?"

I began to dig within myself and notice the barriers I had put up. I found that it wasn't really that I believed that I would never love or be loved again. What I really believed—what I was truly afraid of—was that if I loved you, you would either leave me, or die. I developed this barrier because I had so much loss and abandonment in my past. But now I know that your past is never, ever the reason why you can't have the present and future that you want. I know this, because my sister and I have been able to break free from the past to live the lives we truly desire. We are ordinary women, living extraordinary lives. If we could manifest the lives of our dreams, in spite of our past, we know others can do the same.

I know that some people think that the word *manifest* is woo-woo. But I know that it's true-true! I think about it in relation to my own Christian background. From the beginning of the Bible, there is evidence of our power to manifest what we want. It is a divinely appointed power. I believe God's hand is all over my life in every area of my life. I can feel when I'm trying to push against His hand, and that's when things don't work for me. But when I work with His hand, I can manifest my heart's desires.

When you feel a desire in your heart, know that it was divinely placed there. So if you have a desire, you also have the power to manifest it. Sometimes we allow the past to be the reason why we can't have the present and the future that we want, and that's the only reason why we're not manifesting, or manifesting to the level that we could be.

I mean, think about it: What kind of God would put something in your heart, dangle it like a carrot in front of you, and not allow you to have it? Often, we're so afraid we're not going to get what we want that we make up reasons and justifications and excuses for why that will occur. *This* is what gets to be healed. *This* is where the breakthrough happens. What's waiting on the other side of healing for you? Everything your heart desires!

I wish I could give a percentage of the women we work with who have experienced childhood sexual abuse, but I can't. There's so much shame around it, so much hesitancy to talk about it, that I can't be sure of an exact number, but I know that it's high. There are so many who, even after they've manifested the relationship and the marriage of their dreams, still deal with unhealed trauma. Sometimes it gets triggered with the birth of a child, because so many of the organs involved in creating and birthing a child were the ones that were violated. Other times it gets triggered when they are experiencing intimacy and connection in a safe and loving relationship, because it feels so vulnerable to love and be loved that way. There are still so many who feel like they can't talk about their experiences as children, because talking about it would feel like reliving it. We help people to understand that you're not reliving it, you're just remembering. And we're remembering it so that we can heal it and put it back in the past where it belongs.

One of the very first things that Michelle and I do with our clients is acceptance work. So many people think accepting something means saying it was okay. Or that they're approving or condoning it. All acceptance is is simply acknowledging that what happened, happened. When you haven't taken that step and don't begin to work through it, what you haven't brought acceptance to keeps happening. Similarly harmful scenarios keep happening with different bodies, with different people, and in different relationships. Thinking that not talking about it means that you've gotten over it is a form of resistance, and that resistance keeps intensifying the wounds. When you address it, you're able to heal it.

In our work, Michelle and I talk about Love Barriers. A Love Barrier is a fear, doubt, limiting belief, or dysfunctional pattern. Often, these barriers are generational. They are inherited beliefs. You didn't make them up, but they are a part of you. Some of the biggest blocks are our relationships with ourselves. This impacts love, of course, and because Michelle and I are transformational love coaches, I speak of that aspect of our lives often. But these barriers don't just impact our love lives, they impact our other relationships, and our relationships with money and business. Each aspect of our lives is interconnected with every other aspect, so if there's a barrier that affects one aspect, it affects our lives as a whole. Sometimes, when there's dysfunction in one aspect, such as in our love lives, we throw ourselves into our careers and making money or into our friendships, as a way to not look at or deal with the barrier.

If you have an unhealed relationship with yourself, you'll often find yourself saying, "I can't believe this is happening to me again." I think of this in terms of a weed in a garden. What you see on the surface is the undesirable plant, but the conditions of the soil are what allowed it to grow. When you look underneath the soil, there was something that happened, some sort of deception, some sort of pain, something somebody said, someone you couldn't trust. These conditions form the roots of the weed, which are those self-limiting, self-sabotaging beliefs. Beliefs like, "I can't trust people." Or, "I'm a poor judge of character, and I can't tell who is a good person and who is bad." Or, "I often make big mistakes."

When those roots, those self-limiting beliefs take hold, they color every interaction. Even if you meet someone new, and you're having a wonderful conversation, there's a piece of you that is protected. There's a part that is suspicious. Even if a beautiful friendship forms, you find yourself waiting for the moment where you will be hurt again. Instead of being present in the relationship, you're constantly preparing for the worst. This is why childhood sexual abuse so impacts our adult relationships. That initial betrayal can sow the seeds of "I'm stupid because I trusted somebody," or "I tried to tell someone and got in trouble, so I can't ever be honest with someone again."

So often, children are hurt by someone they loved, somebody they trusted, or someone who their family trusted. It becomes natural to be suspicious of someone who seems trustworthy, or safe, or loving. Going into a relationship, a person wanting to deeply connect with you triggers that suspicion. Even women with children struggle with receiving the unconditional love that their children want to give them, because of these early wounds.

Eventually, after the loss of my first husband, I did my HeartWork™, which takes you through an introspective process that has you clearly see who you are; release yourself from the past, including the fears that may be holding you back; and allows you to discover and access the skills that lead to attracting and experiencing the love and relationship you deserve for the rest of your life! I broke through that fear of not believing I could ever love or be loved again, and I attracted my current husband. I couldn't believe I was in love again. However, even after we were married and had children, he would say to me "You're not with me 100%." And I could not understand what this man was saying.

I was like, "I've given you my heart, my body, children." I felt like he was being selfish. I felt like he was telling me that I needed to give him more, because there was a belief that in love, something was being taken from me. I'm sure that there are others who will resonate here, who have had experiences that felt like intimacy was something being taken from them. So my interpretation was, "You're not giving me enough," where, what my husband was really saying was, "I want to love and be loved by all of you, I want to love all of you."

Part of me was still running, protecting myself, and he could sense it. It was impacting our emotional intimacy, not to mention our physical intimacy. I was terrified that if I loved him completely, he was going to leave or die. I was terrified to love my children with all my heart because I was so scared they were going to die. I wasn't able to love fully and to receive love fully until I did the *HeartWork*™ to break through that fear.

Finally, my coach said to me, "You can either continue waiting for this man to die, or live in love with him."

That day, I decided that if I say "I love you," I love you completely, 100%. Even if that means that one day you might leave me or die. I choose to love you.

I know that people say healing is hard work. And, yes, it is. It can be really uncomfortable. But what is harder is pretending none of this is happening. That there's nothing wrong. To me, *that's* actually hard work. Yes, it's uncomfortable to see what you've been avoiding, but once you stop avoiding it, and once you've healed it, you get to stop doing the hard work of hiding the wound. Of course, you'll always remember what happened to you. But the pain and the suffering and the difficult emotions will disappear. It becomes a thing that happened, something that contributed to me becoming the person that I am today, but it only impacts me in ways that I choose to allow it to impact me.

Part of the power of this choice is that your healing gets to be your own. Notice where you have collapsed someone else's responsibility with your own healing. Partners and loved ones can choose to support you and be there for you, but no one else is required to be part of what is your work to do. Your healing is not contingent on someone else's participation.

My husband knows parts of the sexual trauma I experienced as a young girl, but I really only started to share it with him once I began doing my own healing. I knew that he could love me and support me through the process, but he couldn't do the healing for me. It helped me to share my breakthroughs with him. When things got hard, I also asked him to hold space for me. So, he supported me in doing my healing work, but it was *my* healing work to do.

People feel that in a relationship, you have to share *everything*. I don't think this is necessarily true, which I know is a fairly radical idea to some. You can request support without having to share every detail. You can ask for someone to hold space, or to be held. It is your choice. You get to share what feels important, what feels relevant, and ask for the support you need. Listen to your heart here, really check in with yourself when you decide to share. When sharing things that have happened to me that I have worked to heal, I consider my intention. Why do I want to share this? What do I want this person to know about me? How can I help them see that, if I could get past this and have the life I have, they can, too? I want to share that I am a loving, passionate, courageous woman, and I've overcome so many things. If someone has questions about the things I've overcome, I'm happy to discuss it, but I don't need to share every detail. My intention in telling my story might be clarity. I might want my husband to know that the reason I freeze up when you touch me there is because I am working through a history of sexual abuse. I want him to know that it is not *you*. It is not *your* touch. When I share in this way, my partner now has more clarity, and can better love and support me.

There is so much strength in making active choices around what I share, who gets access to private information, and who doesn't. Not everyone gets the privilege of knowing everything about me. I get to choose which people and in which communities sharing my story feels relevant and nourishing.

Even as you are doing the work to heal, there will be newly uncovered fears and limiting beliefs that come up. Part of the work is to become masterful in breaking through them. You really have to strengthen the muscle of breaking through fears, breaking through limiting beliefs, breaking down dysfunctional patterns, and replacing them with empowering thoughts and beliefs. It is essential to replace these patterns, because, without a new way of being, your brain will simply keep going where it's always gone before. It is important to be resilient when these fears come up. Once you've begun the work, you can notice a fear and not go into a spiral where one fear leads to another and another. When you become masterful at breaking through these fears, they dissipate quickly. Experiencing fear is part of the human condition. Knowing how to break through it is something that once you learn it, and you master it, even if the scariest fear comes up, you'll know that you can get to the other side of it and be in your power.

Your past is simply an informer. It is not a predictor of what's possible for you. I often say that we visit the past with a temporary visa, and then we come right back to the present. We do the work with the past so it doesn't keep impacting our future. You have an incredible power to choose the life you want. You get to be the one to break through a pattern that has been impacting generations. I started to break that pattern when I was seventeen. I didn't know exactly how I was going to do it, but I knew, *this ends with me.* The addiction, the abuse, the abandonment, it ends with me. My children will not have to deal with the same things that I did. And trust me, I was terrified to get married and have children. What if I left my kids? My mom left me, and her mom left her. What if that happened? What if I died, like my dad? But I got to choose. I chose what to cast away, because it didn't serve me, and I chose what to keep as a lesson and a blessing. This choice showed me my power. My unlimited, unbridled, unshakable power.

You have that power, too.

You get to use it in every area of your life.

You *can* create a life and love beyond your wildest dreams.

CHAPTER 15

ME

"The more you say it, the less power it has.
You get to be set free.
You have lived with this long enough!
TIME FUCKING SERVED!"

So . . . here we are! This is the place where I was hoping you and I would end up. I honor you for being brave and courageous. It doesn't matter if you believe in God or not or what you call your source or higher power, but I said a little prayer before I started to write this final chapter so that I could get across how important it is to me that, when you are finished reading these last sentences, you feel inspired and lifted up. It is very important to me that you are filled with hope and peace about who you are. It is important to me that you understand that you are loved and you are not your past. You are not alone. You are perfect. Your life didn't happen "to" you, it happened "for" you.

I know that sounds challenging. How can you wrap your mind around the hurt and the pain that has held you prisoner?

But here I am, hoping to help you to heal from your pain and your shame and tell you that you *can* create a life you love and deserve. I can promise you, we would not be sharing our time together right now if I had not been sexually molested. My story would be different. My life would be different. But I get to be here with you now, looking at my trauma as a gift, and I get to show you how to step out of victimhood and step into creating the life of your dreams.

For years, I prayed for my purpose. It was literally painful for me. I had been running a couple of different businesses that I had tried to scale and grow, but something was always getting in the way. I would come up against obstacle after obstacle, and even though I was blessed and loved what I was doing for work, I knew it was not why I was placed on this Earth.

I always felt like I was in a state of confusion and that I wasn't smart enough to grow my business. It was awful. At that time I was in an organization called Entrepreneurs Organization (EO), and I saw all these magnificent business owners growing their companies, and I always felt like I didn't measure up. I was *always* comparing myself to what they were creating.

Little did I know that God had a way bigger plan for me. I remember watching Oprah Winfrey several years back and I heard her say, "I want to be part of something that is bigger than myself." I actually wrote that down on a post it and put it on my vision board where I would see it from time to time. Be careful what you wish for...

So, there I was . . . feeling stupid and judging myself when I met this friend/mentor, and she told me a few things. She said, "Educate yourself about money and manifesting," and she told me to get very clear on what I wanted. She said that I should say, "I am crystal clear and laser-focused about my purpose in life."

So, I said it, and said it, and said it. Unfortunately, sometimes you don't get the message right away, but the seed had been planted. After I said that mantra, it took about four years for me to have my aha. Then God slapped me upside the head with this book and how I was to share my story. I resisted for about two years. I was like, OH HELL NO! This wasn't a small ask. God wanted me to say, "Yes, I was a little girl who experimented with other children." No one was having this conversation. There was no one to call to ask how to navigate what was to come. There was no one to tell me that everything was going to be okay and that it was all going to work out. I had many obstacles as the book began to unfold. There were legal ramifications that I needed to figure out, and I had to navigate how my family was going to feel about my big reveal. But, because God was the one at the wheel, I started to notice miracles happening and a clearing of the path to make this book a reality. Over and over again, when I was faced with an obstacle, I said, "God . . . this is all you." I just trusted and let go, and now, here we are.

I noticed that when I finally got clear on my purpose, things started to fall into place very quickly. The stars aligned, and things started to happen. As I mentioned, there were legal ramifications that I was extremely nervous about, so I was very hesitant to admit to anything, but God wanted a book. I tentatively began to tell my story in a few safe communities, and all these beautiful people started telling me that my story was their story. These are the brave and courageous people who eventually became the contributors. These are the people who have shared their stories so that you have the evidence to know that you are not alone. This collaboration took some of the pressure off until I could figure out how to safely tell my own story. You got to hear from several people that they, too, acted out. The intentions of this book are about you. It is about your healing. It is about letting go of the shame. It is about showing you that you are not alone.

I want to reiterate and make it very clear that if you were sexually abused, your memories, your experiences, and your journey are yours and yours alone. I would never minimize how you are dealing with it or the massive impact it has had on your life. You may not be ready to forgive. You may have very strong feelings towards that person, but if it was another child—a friend, a babysitter, or a neighbor—I want you to consider that someone probably did it to them, too.

To begin healing, you need to get clear on where your shame stems from. Click or scan here to access a short worksheet that will help you figure out where you feel shame.

Uncover Shame worksheet at
https://unshamed.live/uncovershamebook

If at any time while you are doing this work you feel unsafe and need support, please click or scan this QR code to access a list of places where you can get help.

Resource Center at www.jilleschultz.com/gethelp

Or, go to the Resources Center on page 179 to get help.

Next, you get to accept that it happened. It doesn't mean that what happened to you is right or fair, but once you accept that it happened, you can start to heal. I have done lots of different things to heal my heart. I did therapy, Landmark Education, Heartcore Leadership, hypnosis, reiki, and a form of EMDR. I have also created *7 Critical Steps to Heal From Your Secrets:*

I am not a therapist but these are the steps that helped me through my healing process. Click on the QR Code to download the steps for free.

7 Critical Steps to Heal From Your Secrets at
https://unshamed.live/7stepsBook

Honestly, I don't care what you do, just do *something*. Talk to someone. I promise the story you have made up in your head about what would happen if you told someone is way scarier than reality. Every time I would go to therapy or every time I decided to tell someone, my stomach would be in so many knots. I dreaded the conversation, but every single time I was shocked by the understanding, love, and compassion I received when I did share. You need to get it out of your body. You get to say it out loud. Even if you are just in your bathroom looking in the mirror, you get to say it out loud. Scream it at the top of your lungs, whisper it to yourself. If you want to join a community where you can safely share your story, click or scan here to join my private Facebook group where you can share your story and be with people who have gone through similar trauma.

Living UN-SHAMED Facebook Group

Or Copy and paste to access the Facebook Group.
https://www.facebook.com/groups/223574946905843

Just do it for yourself. The more you say it, the less power it has. You get to be set free. You have lived with this long enough! TIME FUCKING SERVED!

I know this will not happen overnight, but the shame will start to change and fade. I want you to start thinking about what you want. What will make you happy? What is your next step? What is on your heart that you get to have? What do you want to create for your life? I want you to write down five things you really want. Five things that are on your heart. Because you really can have them. You get to bring those things into your life. You get to manifest your dreams into reality.

There was one point in my life many years ago when I finally understood "the secret." I felt like I had been given the keys to the kingdom. I don't remember how it happened or exactly when it happened but all of a sudden, there it was. I realized that I have the power every single day to create my life exactly as I want it. I get to wake up in the morning and say, "What do I want to create for myself? How do I see my life happening for me?" The realization sunk in that if I want to have a toned body, I get to get my ass to the gym. If I want love in my life, I get to put myself out there and put a profile on a dating app. If I want to scale a successful business, I get to learn and study and hire a team to support that. If I want to be president of the US of A . . . you get it. I get to decide every single day what I get to create. It was the biggest truth bomb I have ever had.

When my purpose finally showed up in June of 2022, I stumbled upon Amanda Frances, thought leader, best-selling author, and money queen. In her podcast episode *121: God Gave You Your Desires*, she explained that our desires are our safe guidance and everything in your heart was given to you by God. The trick is to get good at wanting what you want so much that it hurts. Then you get to believe with everything in you that if you want it, it is truly what you are meant to have, and it is your only job every single day to have thoughts all day long to support that. I love her work and if you want additional access to her amazing insights, please click or scan:

Amanda's website at

https://dj613.isrefer.com/go/af/jilleschultz/

I thought to myself, *You mean everything that I want is mine to have? Holy shit!* If this was true, anything I want is mine to have! I have a very long and outrageous list of wants that I now *know* I get to have. Now my day-to-day life has an entirely different purpose. I have created a new morning ritual. I get to wake up and co-create my life with God. I feel so close to God in these moments. This is the time of day when the sun is coming up and the light is spilling through the blinds. The cool air is on my face as I am still bundled up in my warm sheets. I start to buzz with excitement because I know I get to daydream about all of my heart's desires. I get to feel what it feels like to have those things. I know the only reason that I want those things is that God put them on my heart. It's like this little dance we do. I desire it, I feel it happening for me, it gets created, and God and I giggle and laugh. When I leaned into God's plan, I started to believe that I deserved to have all those incredible desires on my heart.

There are two things that go hand in hand when it comes to living a dream life: gratitude and manifesting. You may be leery of manifesting and think it is woo-woo, but it is mentioned several times in the Bible and it is fun as hell.

Gratitude is a very powerful way to manifest more quickly. When you are grateful for the things that you already have in your life, it creates an understanding that we are provided for, we are safe and we have plenty. I also believe that when you are grateful for whatever is going on in your life, even if it is something awful, God can make good come out of it. It is the reason we are together now. I finally got to the place where, even though what happened to me as a little girl was terrible and the pain and shame have sometimes been unbearable, I was able to say, "Thank you God for all of it." Now, I get to share my story with you so that you can see that you are not alone and I can 100% say that it was worth it. If I can help one person get out from under that dark cloud, it is worth the forty-one years it took me to get here.

The fun thing is that you can test God, Spirit, Universe, whatever you have named your higher power, when you are manifesting. God actually likes it when you do. You can ask for a sign around what you're wanting to create. Here is one of the ways I tested this theory. When God first asked me to do this book, I was hesitant. Actually, *hesitant* is an understatement. I was terrified. Terrified to share my story. Terrified to bare my soul. Terrified of what my family and friends would say. Terrified of A LOT of things, and so I said, "God, if this is really what you want me to do, if this is really the path you want me to take, I want to hear Sia's 'Unstoppable.'" It doesn't always happen right away, and it didn't. It actually took a few weeks before I heard the song, but now it has sort of become the anthem for this book. There have been days when I have really wanted out. Days when there have been major roadblocks and I just wanted to lie down and cry, and then that damn song would come on. When I was first confronted with the potential legal complications I have referred to, I went to a very dark place. I mean dark! I knew I needed to tell my story and I knew the book needed to get out there, but I couldn't sacrifice myself and my safety. It was the first time in my life I really had a suicidal thought. I thought, okay, maybe I write the book and then I am just *not here*. I needed to think. I needed to go somewhere where I could get my head on straight, so I headed to the sand and sun and spent some time contemplating my next move. Wouldn't you know it, there was that damn song. Not only did I hear "Unstoppable," a girlfriend with whom I had shared the meaning of the song called me and said she had just heard the song and thought about me. I knew I was on the right path and that God would take care of everything, and time and time again, God continues to do so.

A few months later, on New Year's Eve, I was watching Miley's New Year's Eve Party, and Sia closed the night with the ball drop at midnight. *And she friggin' sang "Unstoppable."* This was an unbelievable moment for me. Sia wrote that song in 2016 so there would be no reason on December 31st, 2022 that she would be promoting that song on any massive stage. But here she was, singing it anyway. God was making a massive gesture just for me that everything that I was doing was divinely planned. There was no misunderstanding that this book was going to mean something. This book was going to help people. The feelings were overwhelming, and I completely lost it. I sobbed and sobbed. My girlfriend thought I had lost my mind, but it may have been one of the most beautiful moments I have ever had in my life. God was giving me a massive sign. This was clarity and confirmation that it was all going to be okay and everything was going to work out. Even though I still wonder why God picked me, I have so much gratitude. Hopefully, you can start to see your trauma as a gift and you too can make a difference in someone's life by saying it out loud.

You are worth the work to heal. Do the work. Regardless of what happened to you, a beautiful life gets to be yours. You get to move on. You get to forgive and to be forgiven. You get to love yourself. You have been in pain long enough, and you get to close that chapter now. Your time in pain and shame has been served, and you get to be released from it. You get to move forward and create the life of your dreams.

With love,

Jill

God's prayer for me (that I now share with you):

You have arrived, my dear. You have worked so hard to get here, and now you get to feel safe, loved, appreciated, powerful, vulnerable and free. You get to be at peace.

Love,

God

ABOUT THE AUTHOR

Jill E. Schultz is a serial entrepreneur, industry disruptor, author, motivational speaker and business strategist. After years of praying for her purpose, she finally realized her life's work is to release people from shame and change the lens through which people see how children who have been sexually abused innocently and curiously experiment with other children. In her courageous work around her own healing, she has been able to let go of the debilitating shame and self-loathing that had kept her paralyzed for forty-one years. The realization that most helped her out of this shame was that she was not alone. That so many others had similar experiences became both a powerful source of light on her own path, and a call to action to share her story. Jill brings this taboo topic out of the shadows so that people can overcome their shame and live the life of their dreams. Jill's warmth, understanding, lived experience and quick wit diffuse some of the heaviness around this subject. Jill is an expert in shame, and if there were degrees (associate's, bachelor's, master's, PhD, double PhD) in shame, she'd have them all. Whether you have suffered from sexual abuse or have a secret, any kind of secret, Jill's approach to releasing any kind of shame will leave you free to create a space for love, success, and abundance.

RESOURCES

RAINN (Rape, Abuse & Incest National Network)
GET HELP 24/7 | CALL 800.656.HOPE (4673)
www.rainn.org

Survivors of Incest Anonymous
(877)-SIA-WS01 or (877) 742-9761
https://siawso.org

Celebrate Recovery
admin@cr-connected.com
www.celebraterecovery.com

Overeaters Anonymous
https://oa.org/
Tel 505-891-2664

National Domestic Violence Hotline
800-799-SAFE (7233)
https://www.thehotline.org/

National Children's Advocacy Center
256-533-KIDS(5437) or 256-534-6883
https://www.nationalcac.org/

Child Abuse Hotline
(1-800) 4-A-Child 800-422-4453
https://www.childhelp.org/hotline/

Sex Trafficking Prevention and Intervention
https://www.childwelfare.gov/

National Suicide Prevention Hotline
800-273-8255 or 988
https://suicidepreventionlifeline.org/

NO MORE Global Directory
https://nomoredirectory.org/